P9-AOH-499

Leading Leaders

Also by Jeswald W. Salacuse:

The Global Negotiator: Making, Managing, and Mending Deals Around the World in the Twenty-First Century

The Wise Advisor: What Every Professional Should Know About Consulting and Counseling

Making Global Deals: Negotiating in the International Market Place

The Art of Advice: How to Give It and How to Take It

International Business Planning: Law and Taxation (with W. P. Streng, six volumes)

An Introduction to Law in French-Speaking Africa: North Africa

An Introduction to Law in French-Speaking Africa: Africa South of the Sahara

Nigerian Family Law (with A. B. Kasunmu)

Leading Leaders

How to Manage Smart, Talented, Rich, and Powerful People

Jeswald W. Salacuse

AMACOM

American Management Association

New York • Atlanta • Brussels • Chicago • Mexico City • San Francisco
Shanghai • Tokyo • Toronto • Washington, D. C.

Special discounts on bulk quantities of AMACOM books are available to corporations, professional associations, and other organizations. For details, contact Special Sales Department, AMACOM, a division of American Management Association, 1601 Broadway, New York, NY 10019.
Tel.: 212-903-8316. Fax: 212-903-8083.
Web site: www.amacombooks.org

This publication is designed to provide accurate and authoritative information in regard to the subject matter covered. It is sold with the understanding that the publisher is not engaged in rendering legal, accounting, or other professional service. If legal advice or other expert assistance is required, the services of a competent professional person should be sought.

Library of Congress Cataloging-in-Publication Data

Salacuse, Jeswald W.
   Leading leaders : how to manage smart, talented, rich, powerful people / Jeswald W. Salacuse.
      p.   cm.
   Includes bibliographical references and index.
   ISBN 0-8144-1766-3
   1. Leadership.   2. Elite (Social sciences)   I. Title.

HD57.7.S239   2006
658.4'092—dc22   2005012243

© 2006 Jeswald W. Salacuse.
All rights reserved.
Printed in the United States of America.

This publication may not be reproduced, stored in a retrieval system, or transmitted in whole or in part, in any form or by any means, electronic, mechanical, photocopying, recording, or otherwise, without the prior written permission of AMACOM, a division of American Management Association, 1601 Broadway, New York, NY 10019.

Printing number

10   9   8   7   6   5   4   3   2   1

FOR JACK

CONTENTS

PREFACE

I FIRST BEGAN to think seriously about the subject of leadership in May 1980 when I was appointed dean of the School of Law of Southern Methodist University in Dallas, Texas. After the university's president James Zumberg offered me the job and I had accepted, he proceeded to give me what I later came to call the "leadership speech," a pep talk that tells a newly appointed leader the wonderful things that are expected to happen under his or her leadership. As President Zumberg expressed his confidence that the law school's faculty would be strengthened, the student body improved, and the endowment increased under *my leadership*, I remember thinking, "What is this man talking about?"

Leadership was just not a word I associated with myself. Leadership was what Winston Churchill did in World War II, what Martin Luther King did during the civil rights movement, and what John F. Kennedy did in launching the New Frontier. It had not occurred to me that leadership was something that would be required of me at SMU. Manage, yes. Administer, sure. But lead? During the course of that interview, two questions first came to mind that I have continued to think about to this day: What is leadership? And how do you do it? Over the next twenty-five years in various other leadership positions and in my own research, I looked for answers to those two questions. This book is the product of that exploration.

My experience as the dean of two graduate schools over fifteen years, as president or chairman of three national professional and academic organizations, as lead director on several corporate boards, as president of an international arbitration tribunal, and as a consultant to governments, institutions, and companies in over thirty countries, taught me that many traditional ideas about leading people did not seem to apply to what I did. For example, some discussions about leadership either explicitly or implicitly draw on military experience or analogies. The people to be led are "troops" whom the leader, like a charismatic general, has to mobilize, energize, and direct. Other commentators liken leaders to sports team coaches whose job it is to inspire their "players" to work together and to give their utmost for the sake of the team.

In fact, the people I led were not troops or players in any sense of the word. Whether they were tenured university professors, corporate board members, international arbitrators, research scientists, wealthy donors, successful lawyers, or government officials, I came to realize that the people I was supposed to lead were themselves leaders. They were leaders because their talents, knowledge, wealth, and network of contacts gave them their own followers, supporters, and constituencies, a factor that was crucial to leading them successfully.

As I examined other organizations in my research, I came to see the same phenomenon: investment banks, law and accounting firms, corporate boards, research organizations, and consulting companies were filled with leaders. Persons who managed those organizations had the fundamental task of leading leaders, not mobilizing troops or inspiring athletes. Successful leadership of many organizations requires leaders, right from the start, to recognize that they are leading leaders and to develop their strategies and plans accordingly. The purpose of this book is to explain this approach to leadership and to guide managers who more often than not will find themselves leading leaders.

In writing this book, I am indebted to literally hundreds of persons whom I had the privilege of leading and learning from over the past twenty-five years. Unfortunately, space limitations prevent me from mentioning them by name. I would, however, especially like to thank Deborah Vouche-Barrelet, my research assistant, for her invaluable work on this project, and Donna Booth Salacuse, who once again gave me the benefit of her superb editorial judgment and skill.

Jeswald W. Salacuse

Leading Leaders

LEADERS AS FOLLOWERS

I must follow the people. Am I not their leader?

—BENJAMIN DISRAELI

UNLESS YOU ARE a total megalomaniac, you recognize, readily or grudgingly, that many of the people you are supposed to lead are smarter, more talented, richer, or more powerful than you are. They are not the faceless, docile "middle managers," "troops," or "team members" so often the subject of books and lectures on leadership. Many of the people you lead, whether you like it or not, are themselves leaders.

Leading Without Authority

The challenge of leading leaders arises in a multiplicity of situations and contexts in modern life, but it is particularly present in managing high-talent organizations, organizations that have high concentrations of persons whose levels of education, skill, wealth, and influence are substantially above the average of the general population. Managers of virtually all personal service firms face the challenge every day as they seek to lead lawyers, management consultants, physicians, investment bankers, research analysts, accountants, and portfolio managers, to name just a few, whose talents are the firm's principal assets and who as partners may also be the firm's owners. Even if they are

1

not technically partners in an organization, their vital skills and talents often give them what amounts to a proprietary role in the firm's activities.

Heads of academic institutions, research organizations, and think tanks face a similar challenge in leading tenured professors, scientists, and scholars. How, for example, should the president of a university persuade tenured professors, who by law cannot be fired or demoted and who have distinguished international reputations and lucrative private consulting practices, to support new programs and teach new courses that are in the best interests of the university? How should administrators of hospitals and health maintenance organizations induce individualistic, highly skilled doctors and medical specialists to initiate more efficient ways of practicing medicine? No amount of military analogies or sports images is likely to facilitate either of these tasks.

The challenge of leading leaders is not confined to high-talent organizations. It is also found in traditional corporations. As companies hire persons because of their special knowledge and skills, managing them may seem more akin to managing a personal services firm, think tank, or academic institution than a traditional hierarchical corporation. In addition, all chief executives in both the business and the nonprofit worlds have the task of effectively leading their organizations' board of directors or governing body. This too is basically a job of leading leaders, since these boards consist of independent individuals who have been chosen precisely because of their achievements, reputations, connections, wealth, or special expertise.

What characterizes all of these situations is that persons designated as leaders, whether they are university presidents, managing partners, or CEOs, have limited authority over the persons they are supposed to lead. Authority, for purposes of this discussion, is the right by virtue of one's position to direct the activities of other persons— in short, to tell them what to do. The challenge for these leaders is unlike that presented in many leadership books in which CEOs or other corporate leaders have full authority over the persons they lead.

While the managing partner of a law firm or the president of a think tank may have some limited legal authority over persons in their organizations, many other situations call upon individuals to lead others over whom they have no real authority whatsoever. Chairpersons, presidents, and presiding officers of committees, commissions, boards, courts, and numerous other deliberative bodies at every level from a village zoning commission to the United States Senate face the challenge on a daily basis.

Effective leadership usually means the difference between accomplishing and failing at that body's tasks. As minority leader and then majority leader of the Senate in the 1950s, Lyndon Johnson had no real authority over other senators, each of whom was a leader with a distinct power base. Senate committee chairpersons, chosen because of their seniority, controlled Senate activity, not the individual designated as the party's leader in the Senate. Before Johnson, party leaders who sought to impose their authority over other senators had failed, usually in humiliating ways. Yet Johnson, through skilled leadership strategies and tactics, effectively imposed his will on Senate Democrats and caused them to pass important measures that they had refused in the past. His leadership skills made him "master of the Senate."[1]

A hundred and fifty years earlier, U.S. Supreme Court Justice John Marshall laid the foundations for constitutional government in the United States not only through his legal ability, but through his equally important skill at leading the other Supreme Court justices to forge unanimous opinions on key issues—much to the consternation of Marshall's political enemy, President Thomas Jefferson, who had appointed many of the justices who seemed so willing to join Chief Justice Marshall in his decisions.[2] It puzzled and frustrated Jefferson that the Supreme Court justices—some of whom were his political allies—who had lifetime appointments to the Court, who were leaders in law and politics in their own right, and over whom Marshall had no real authority—seemed so willing to follow Marshall's lead on important constitutional questions. In effect, President Jefferson was asking the basic question that this book addresses: How was it that Chief Justice Marshall, with no real authority over the other justices of the Supreme Court, was able to lead leaders so effectively?

Lack of authority does not necessarily mean lack of power. If power means the ability to determine the course of events, then clearly both Marshall and Johnson had the power that made them effective leaders in their organizations. Similarly, persons called upon to lead other leaders may have limited legal authority to direct their associates' actions, but through various strategies and tactics discussed in this book they may gain the ability—the

> Lack of authority does not necessarily mean lack of power.

power—to cause other leaders to act in desired ways for the benefit of the organization.

In seeking to understand leadership, scholars and commentators have looked for useful analogies and guidance in sports and the military. When it comes to leading leaders, these fields are of limited use because they usually assume a structure of authority that simply does not exist in high-talent organizations. Rather, the field of politics, both national and international, where authority is often vague and even nonexistent, offers much better lessons for leading leaders. As a result, this book will draw heavily on the experience of political leadership to illustrate its approach.

Leaders as a Different Breed of Cat

Leaders in various organizations, professions, and walks of life, are often referred to as "elites." While the term "elite" has negative connotations for many people in this democratic age, it refers to a vast and diverse group of individuals who, because of their education, talents, wealth, or power, are able to exert significant, usually disproportionate influence within their organizations and in society generally. One simple definition of an *elite* is a person who has "more"—more education, more talent, more money, and more clout than the rest of us. Their knowledge, skills, money, or power give elites a special role in their organizations and often gain them special privileges, whether their managers and other employees like it or not. Elites are not troops that readily fall into line behind their leader, no matter how charismatic that person may be. They are themselves leaders.

The literature on leadership is long, but little research has focused on the challenge of leading leaders. Definitions of leadership abound in that literature, but for present purposes we define leadership as "the ability to cause other persons to act in desired ways for the benefit of an organization or group." From that perspective, trying to lead leaders is like herding cats, and one must admit that elite followers in organizations are indeed a different breed of cat in several respects.

• First, elites' brains, talents, wealth, and power always mean that they have many options outside the organization and that those options give them a strong sense of independence from both the organization and its leader. As C. Wright Mills wrote in his classic study of elites, "they are not made by their jobs . . . they can escape."[3] Their special gifts and attributes also mean that the organization needs them and may find it difficult to replace them. Consequently, an important challenge for leaders of elites is to prevent them from escaping.

• Second, in many high-talent organizations—such as investment banks, consulting firms, and academic institutions—elites have a formal or informal proprietary interest in the institution and often have played a role in choosing their leader; consequently, they often believe that the leader is beholden to them and not the other way around.

• Third, elites have their own followers and constituencies, whose loyalties and respect they value and who therefore are powerful influences on their behavior. Indeed, they depend on those constituencies in order to hold on to their positions as elites. For example, you will have little success in leading politicians, labor officials, community organizers, and department heads unless you understand the interests and attitudes of the persons they represent.

• Fourth, elites often have powerful loyalties to institutions outside the organization where they work, and the signals they receive from those outside institutions often influence them more than anything the leader can do and say. For example, university professors and research scientists have strong loyalties to their professional disciplines and colleagues throughout the world. The kudos and criticism they receive from those professional and disciplinary institutions and colleagues may have a far more potent effect on their behavior than anything their university president or dean might do or say.

• Fifth, elites do not conceive of themselves as followers. They see themselves as leaders and they want to be treated as such. They are therefore quick to challenge or belittle anything that suggests that they are being led. Traditional symbols of leadership such as stirring speeches, emotional appeals to action, and directives from the top are likely to fall on deaf ears or, worse yet, become the subject of ridicule.

• Finally, because of their special value to their organizations, elites believe that they are entitled to special benefits and privileges that other persons in the organization do not have, and they constantly seek to negotiate with the organization and its leaders to obtain them.

In addition to persons who fit the traditional definition of an elite, you may find leaders throughout any organization, at all levels, whether or not they have an office in the executive suite or a seat on the governing board. An administrative assistant in an office and a mechanic on the shop floor may qualify as leaders because of their disproportionate influence over co-workers who look to them for advice, guidance, and yes, leadership.

The skills for effectively leading this different breed of cat are significantly different from those used in more traditional corporate organizations. Otherwise successful leaders who do not understand this difference have encountered serious problems and even failures in managing elites. For example, an American banker, who had for ten years successfully managed a medium-sized European bank in London, decided for family reasons to return to the United States and take a position as the executive head of an investment advisory firm whose clients consisted of wealthy individuals. Instead of leading a team of buttoned-down bank executives, he now had to manage a group of thirty eccentric portfolio managers, all of whom had doctoral degrees in finance or mathematics. His management style, which had been so effective in London, proved to be a source of discontent and eventual rebellion in San Francisco. He left the firm after six months.

In the nonprofit world, an experienced executive conceived and established an innovative organization to provide technical assistance to developing countries. He proved to be an effective entrepreneur in raising funds, hiring staff, and developing programs. After fifteen years, he decided to seek a new challenge and so became the executive director of an established organization whose staff consisted of highly trained specialists with long-standing ties to members of the organization's board of directors. He arrived with a new vision for the organization that was then having significant financial problems. Relying on his entrepreneurial, proprietary style of operation that had served him so well in his first organization, he moved rapidly to implement his new vision, but ran into a brick wall of resistance from the organization's specialists who objected that they had not been consulted. Eventually, a delegation from the organization's board asked him to resign.

> You find leaders at all levels throughout any organization, whether or not they have an office in the executive suite or a seat on the governing board.

Also in the nonprofit world, as we will see later in Chapter Five, Lawrence Summers, a former U.S. Secretary of the Treasury, ran into the same kind of problem when he was appointed President of Harvard University in 2002. From the outset, his use of an assertive management style, better suited to a government department or old-fashioned corporation, to lead the Harvard faculty, *all of whom considered themselves leaders*, resulted in serious friction. Ultimately, in 2005, a faculty vote of no-confidence put his presidency in jeopardy.

Leading Leaders Against Iraq

Two significant and instructive efforts to lead leaders occurred in 1990–1991 and again in 2003, when the United States went to war against Iraq. The first was a success, the second a failure. In 1990–1991, when Iraq invaded and occupied Kuwait, George H. W. Bush, the 41st President of the United States, skillfully organized and led a broad international coalition of nations and that drove Iraq from Kuwait with United Nations approval. That coalition did not automatically and spontaneously spring into existence. To create it, President Bush had to lead the leaders of the world's most important countries.

Twelve years later, his son, George W. Bush, the 43rd President of the United States, believing that the removal of Saddam Hussein from power in Iraq was in the United States' vital interests, also sought to put together a broad international coalition and secure United Nation authorization for military action against Iraq. He failed to achieve either. While the two situations were different with respect to the historical moment, international dynamics of the day, and the problems the two men faced, the fact remains that Bush the father was successful at leading leaders but Bush the son was not. In comparing the two situations, a natural and important question is *why* the father succeeded but the son failed.

French-Fried Leadership

For many supporters of George W. Bush, the answer to that question is easy: the French. France, displaying its traditional anti-American-ism and thinking only of its own short-term, selfish interests, not only refused to join the American coalition against in Iraq in 2003 but also mobilized other countries in their opposition to American efforts. As a result, politicians and talk radio hosts thundered against the cowardly, perfidious, ungrateful French. After all, hadn't the United States liberated them from Nazi Germany in World War II? So wasn't it natural for Americans to show displeasure by boycotting French wines and even changing the name of French fries to "freedom fries," as was done on certain menus, including one in a restaurant at the Capitol building in Washington, D.C.?

But before accepting that facile explanation, one should ask whether it is not merely a case of a leader blaming followers for his own failure of leadership. Unsuccessful leaders have a tendency to blame their followers for their own failings, so one must be careful in accepting their explanations. Surely, directors or shareholders of a corporation having trouble integrating a company that it had acquired would not be convinced by the CEO's explanation that it was all the fault of middle managers who refused to "get with the program." Similarly, a board of trustees of a university or hospital found guilty of broad scale, long-standing sexual harassment of its female employees would not be likely to accept the President's explanation that the problem lay essentially with professors and doctors who simply would not pay attention to his numerous memos and pronouncements on the need to treat female employees fairly.

Failures of an organization or a country to achieve desired results, whether in integrating other companies, assuring nondiscrimination in the workplace, or gaining support for its foreign policy, lie as often in mistakes of leadership as in the intractable structure of the situation. Indeed, one of the tasks of great leaders is to change the apparently intractable structure of a situation in order to achieve desired results for the organization or country. A closer examination of

the conduct of George H. W. Bush in 1990-1991 and of his son in
2003 leads one to conclude that the father's success was as much
attributable to his leadership qualities and actions as to the situation,
and that the inability of his son to lead leaders into a broad coalition
against Iraq was as much attributable to his ineffective leadership
qualities and actions as it was to the intractable French.

A Contrast in Leadership

A comparison of the two cases illustrates some important lessons
about the challenges of and the useful approaches to leading leaders.
First, President George H. W. Bush strongly believed that if other
nations were to join the coalition to drive Iraq from Kuwait, the
United States had to take an active, energetic leadership role in convincing them to join. He truly believed their participation was essential for the success of any effort against Iraq. Leadership, in his view,
required diplomacy across a broad front, and he proceeded to orchestrate a complex diplomatic effort at many levels—through direct contacts with the leaders themselves, through diplomatic missions by his
deputies, through action at the United Nations and other international organizations, through foreign embassies in the United States,
and through American ambassadors abroad—to build and maintain a
coalition of nations united in their efforts to drive Iraq from Kuwait.
All of this preceded his initiation of military action. George H. W.
Bush's leadership was based on persuasion before action.[4]

In contrast to the importance attached to and the determination
to create a coalition in 1990-1991 by President George H. W. Bush,
the prevailing attitude in many parts of his son's administration
twelve years later was that other countries had no choice but to follow
the United States. For George W. Bush and his associates in 2003,
leadership by the United States seemed to flow automatically from its
status as the world's only superpower. Moreover, if other countries
did not follow the United States into war against Iraq, the Bush ad-

ministration declared publicly that the United States would go to war alone, not a strong message signaling the importance of creating a coalition.

So in 2002-2003, President George W. Bush and members of his administration talked about "a coalition of the willing," as if that coalition would come into existence simply though the desire of other countries to join it and without the need for the United States to actively work to create a coalition through international leadership. The prevailing attitude of the Bush administration was that unilateral action by the United States would lead to multilateral action by other countries, not that multilateral diplomacy should come first. If the United States acted decisively, others would follow, a view summed up by two authors as the "if you build it, they will come" doctrine, which expressed the belief that the United States was a unique country not just in terms of its power but also its moral authority for using that power.[5]

As things turned out, of course, many countries—such as France, Germany, Turkey, and Egypt, who had participated in the war to liberate Kuwait in 1991, as well as long-time allies such as Canada and Mexico—refused to go to war against Iraq in 2003. One lesson to be drawn from this aspect of the comparison of the two cases is that other leaders, in their capacity as followers, always have options not to follow you, and that leadership is not an automatic process that happens because of your status or resources. Rather, leadership (particularly of other leaders) is a willed, deliberate activity to which even the strongest leaders must devote assiduous effort. In short, if you want to lead other people, especially other leaders, you have to work at it.

A second important difference between the two situations is that Bush the father had broad experience in international diplomacy and long-standing relationships with the leaders of the day. As Vice President for eight years, U.S. ambassador to the United Nations, director of the CIA, and ambassador to China, the 41st President of the United States intimately understood how international diplomacy worked and was on a first-name basis with national leaders throughout the world. In putting together his successful coalition, he relied on his vast experience and contacts, and he energetically and personally contacted the leaders concerned by telephone, often on a daily basis, an approach that caused some members of his staff to call him "the mad dialer."

Bush the son, on the other hand, whose only previous government position was as governor of Texas, had no diplomatic experience and did not personally know the leaders he was seeking to lead into the coalition. Rather than deal personally with foreign leaders, as his father had done, he often delegated that task to other members of his administration, notably to Secretary of State Colin Powell, and later to United Kingdom Prime Minister Tony Blair. Rather than communicate one-on-one to persuade reluctant European leaders to follow him, George W. Bush often conveyed his messages through the media, a fact that tended to annoy the leaders he was seeking to lead.

Even Bush's deputies did not actively undertake energetic efforts to lead other countries into the coalition. For example, whereas President George H. W. Bush's Secretary of States James Baker visited forty-one countries on five continents to help forge a coalition for the Gulf War, Colin Powell hardly traveled anywhere in the months prior to the Iraq war. Two scholars summed up the situation: "Powell would later claim that modern technology like e-mail and telephones rendered personal diplomacy less important than it used to be, and that he saw his European counterparts frequently at UN meetings in New York during this period. But that view understates both the symbolic and practical importance of personal engagement on the ground in the foreign countries themselves. By limiting contacts with key allies in Europe, the Bush administration only reinforced the impression that they had little interest in or respect for the views of others, and that matters of war and peace were for Washington to decide."[6]

From this dimension of the comparison of the two cases, one draws further important lessons about leading leaders. First, leadership is not a matter of position but of relationships. To be a leader, you need followers, and followers choose to follow a particular leader because of their relationship with him or her. Second, one-on-one, personal encounters are vital in building the relationships needed to lead leaders.

The reason relationships are important in leading leaders is not because of the warm feeling they engender. Rather, it is that they have an important function in the leadership process. Positive relationships engender trust, and trust in a leader is vital in securing desired action from followers. Any proposed action by a leader entails risk. Persons perceive that following a course of action proposed by a leader whom they trust is less risky and therefore more acceptable than following the same recommended course of action by a leader whom they do not trust. World leaders, because of their personal relationship with and resulting trust in President George H. W. Bush, were more disposed to follow him than his son, with whom they did not have a personal relationship.

A third important factor in comparing the two cases is the importance of understanding and giving deference to the interests of the persons you lead. People follow you because they believe it is in their interests to do so. They don't follow you just because you claim to be a leader, because others have designated you as leader, or because you have the resources and position of leadership. In 1990–1991, George H. W. Bush understood the interests of the world leaders he was seeking to lead and sought to accommodate those interests as he forged a coalition to drive Iraq from Kuwait. The world leaders of the day wanted the United Nations to be heavily involved and believed that United Nations authorization was vital. They believed it was in their interests to seek multilateral solutions to serious international problems. They also needed a clear rationale for going to war against Iraq. Both of these elements were important if the leaders of coalition countries were to convince their own citizens on the rightness of being part of a coalition in a war against Iraq.[7] A further interest for many European and Arab countries was a solution to the Israeli-Palestinian conflict. Accordingly, President George H. W. Bush accommodated these interests in his strategy of coalition formation by emphasizing the importance of the United Nations, by pursuing diplomatic processes before embarking on military action, by emphasizing the single overriding reason for war, which was the clear violation of an independent nation's sovereignty, the United Nations Charter, and basic principles of international law, and by promising to launch a new diplomatic initiative to solve the Palestinian problem once Iraq was driven from Kuwait. Furthermore, he promised certain leaders substantial aid packages in return for their participation in the coalition. Thus, throughout the buildup to the Gulf War, George H. W. Bush constantly sought to engage other leaders, to understand the interests that drove them, to listen to their objections and concerns, and to seek a means to accommodate those interests while pursuing his own overriding goal of building a coalition.

On the other hand, President George W. Bush in 2003 seemed to have little concern for the interests of potential coalition partners and did little to accommodate those interests to get them to follow him. While seeking their support, he showed little regard for the United Nations, an institution that most countries felt was important for their diplomatic interests. Moreover, he was openly contemptuous of a multilateral approach to international diplomacy, having previously withdrawn the United States from the Kyoto Protocol and the 1972 Anti-Ballistic Missile Treaty, as well as rejecting outright the new International Criminal Court. Bush administration officials often made public statements that seemed to indicate that the interests of other nations were not important: "Either you are with us or you are with the terrorists," and "If you don't go with us, we will go alone."

> People follow you because they believe it is in their interests to do so.

Similarly, the United States' constantly changing rationales for the War—the removal of weapons of mass destruction, the elimination of Iraq as a base for Al Qaeda terrorists, or the liberation of the Iraqi people from tyranny—made it difficult for other leaders to sell the war to their own people. Moreover, active support of Israeli Prime Minister Sharon's aggressive policies towards the Palestinians gave little deference to European interests on that particular question.

Unlike his father, George W. Bush did not actively engage other world leaders, did not take their interests seriously, and did not seek to accommodate them. Indeed, he tended to view the objections of France, Germany, and other skeptics of American policy as ingratitude and disloyalty, as self-serving actions that could only be explained by base motives. Rather than engage these skeptics as his father had done, he chose to ignore them, isolate them, and ultimately ostracize them diplomatically, to the point that the Air Force One menu started offering "freedom toast" for breakfast.

Conclusion: Lessons for Leading Leaders

Comparing the two efforts to lead leaders against Iraq, one can identify five principal lessons that help to explain President George H. W. Bush's success. While you may never be called upon to build a coalition of sovereign states, these lessons can offer you helpful insights in carrying out your leadership role in situations that require you to lead other leaders. The five lessons are:

1. Your ability to lead other leaders arises not just from your position, resources, or charisma but from your will and skill. If you want to lead other persons, especially leaders, you have to work at the job.

2. The basis of leadership, particularly with other leaders, is your relationship with the persons you lead. Trust in the leader is a necessary element of leadership, and persons are more disposed to follow a leader in whom they have trust than one they do not trust.

3. Communication is your fundamental tool in building those relationships.

4. The key process of leading leaders is communication through one-on-one interactions with the persons you would lead. If you lead other leaders, you have to engage them and personally connect with them.

5. In developing your leadership strategies and tactics, you need to take account of the interests of the persons you would lead. Leading leaders is above all interest-based leadership. Leaders will follow you not because of your position or charisma but because they consider it in their interest. Your job as a leader is to convince them that their interests lie with you.

In the following chapters we will see how to apply these lessons to leading leaders in a variety of other areas and organizations.

Notes

1. See generally, Robert Caro, *The Years of Lyndon Johnson: Master of the Senate* (New York: Alfred A. Knopf, 2002).

2. Jean Edward Smith, *John Marshall: Definer of a Nation* (New York: Henry Holt, 1996), p. 448.

3. C. Wright Mills, *The Power Elite* (New York: Oxford University Press, 1956), p. 3.

4. For a detailed description of the actions taken to build the coalition prior to the Gulf War, see Susan Rosegrant and Michael Watkins, "The Gulf Crisis: Building a Coalition for War" (Cambridge, Mass.: J. F. Kennedy School of Government Case Program, C16-94-1264.0, 1994).

5. Philip H. Gordon and Jeremy Shapiro (The Brookings Institution), *Allies at War* (New York: McGraw-Hill, 2004), p. 50.

6. Ibid, pp. 173-174.

7. Referring to the Bush administration's changing reasons for going to war ("WMD, Axis of Evil, Bringing Democracy"), former Secretary of State Madeleine Albright has written: "By complicating its own

choice, the administration has instead complicated the choices faced by others, divided Europe, and played into the hands of extremists who would like nothing better than to make the clash of civilizations the defining struggle of our age." Madeleine K. Albright, "Bridges, Bombs, or Blusters?" in *Foreign Affairs*, (September-October 2003), p. 18.

LEADING ONE-ON-ONE

> The shepherd always tries to persuade the sheep that their interests and his own are the same.
>
> —STENDHAL

THE SEARCH FOR the meaning of leadership has become the modern alchemy of organizational management. Although everyone agrees that leadership is important, indeed vital, for the success of organizations, a clear understanding of its nature has eluded scholars and practitioners just as the means for turning lead into gold eluded medieval alchemists. Some scholars have sought to explain leaders and leadership in terms of leaders' personal characteristics; others have focused on their modes of behavior; and still others have looked for its essence in the situations that give rise to effective leadership. While fashions of interpreting leadership have changed from time to time, no one has yet seriously suggested that leadership study be abandoned the way alchemy finally was.[1]

Defining Leadership

"Leadership" expresses a complex and at the same time flexible concept that has allowed scholars and practitioners to define it in many ways. The English word "leader" is derived from the old English *lae-*

dan, which meant to show the way, to be ahead of—a word that conjured up images of shepherds walking in front of their flocks in order to lead them to a particular destination. It also implies the notion of the sheep willingly following the shepherd. In this respect, it is to be distinguished from the idea of driving a herd of cattle from the rear by using force. Leadership also suggests the action of showing the way, of moving a group of people willing toward an objective.

Many languages, including French and Spanish, have no precise equivalent for the English words "leader" or "leadership." As a result, the English words for these terms have found their way into those languages. So French books and articles on politics and management often refer to "le leader," and French libraries have titles like *"Comment Trouver Le Leader en Vous"* ("How to Find the Leader in You") and *"Le Leader de Demain"* ("The Leader of Tomorrow"). In Spanish, the word *el lider,* which seems to have supplanted the more indigenous *"jefe,"* is also derived from the English.

Leadership implies the existence of followers. To be a leader you need persons who will follow you. One person alone on a desert island could never be a leader. The arrival on that island of another survivor from a shipwreck creates the potential for leadership. Not only does leadership require the presence of other persons, it also requires that those persons be willing to follow the leader in an indicated direction.

Leadership, as we understand it today, is of course much more than merely showing the way. Its also implies the ability to persuade or cause persons to whom the way is shown to actually move willingly in that direction. The test of leadership is followership. History is filled with prophets who have tried to show the way but have failed to move their potential flocks. We may revere their wisdom today and lament the ignorance of those who rejected them, but we cannot say they were leaders. They were not leaders precisely because no one would follow them. To be a leader, you must have the ability to cause other persons to move in the direction that you want them to go. As we saw in Chapter 1, leadership is not accidental, but a willed, deliberate activity.

> The test of leadership is followership.

For purposes of this book, we have defined leadership as "the ability to cause individuals to act willingly in a desired way for the benefit of a group." The precise action desired of followers will vary according to the situation and the circumstances. In his seminal study, *Leadership*, James MacGregor Burns drew a fundamental distinction between *transactional leadership*, which seeks to lead others by mediating among their competing interests, and *transformational* leadership, which leads people by changing their attitudes and beliefs.[2] Whether leadership is transactional or transformational, it raises some fundamental questions: Where does the ability to lead others come from? What precisely does it consist of? How may a person acquire it?

Scholars and writers on leadership, like medieval alchemists, have traditionally sought to find the source of this special quality. For some writers, leadership is a skill honed through practice and study. For others it is a rare, natural talent, like artistic ability, that a person is born with. Still others equate it with a particular position and the authority that goes with it. For yet others, it is a unique energy that a few gifted individuals possess but most others lack. Finally, a different school of thought holds that leadership does not arise from personal characteristics at all, but from situations. Leadership is situational.[3] A person who is an effective leader in one situation, for example as CEO of a multinational corporation, could prove to be a disaster in another situation, say as president of a university. The multiplicity of explanations only serves to complicate the search for leadership's essence.

Leadership as Relationship

My own experience and observations have led me to conclude that the essence of leadership—of leadership in action—is not a quality at all. It is a relationship—a relationship between a leader and the persons led. It is the existence of that relationship that causes persons to act in ways indicated by the leader as being beneficial to the group. The basis of any relationship is some perceived *connection* that exists between leader and follower. The nature of that connection varies with time and circumstance. It may be psychological, economic, or political. Whatever its basis, leaders work hard at creating that connection because they know that effective leadership depends on it. Whether a leader in Burns' terminology is transactional or transformative, underlying the ability to lead is the existence of a relationship, a connection, with the persons to be led.

Relationships enable leadership because they often contain two vital forces that move people: trust and self-interest. The relationship between leader and follower often tends to create trust in the leader. Trust, as we shall see, is essential to leadership. People do not follow persons whom they do not trust, and a person cannot develop trust in another person without coming to know that person. Taking action to follow any leader always creates risk, uncertainty, and vulnerability, whether that action is a corporate restructuring, an invasion of a foreign country, or merely a decision to hire an unorthodox professor at a university. Having trust in the leader allows followers to accept the proposed action more readily than if no trust existed because trust in the leader has the effect of reducing the perceived risk and uncertainty in the proposed course of action.

In addition to trust, self-interest arising out of relationships can also facilitate leadership. Many relationships entail a mutual flow of benefits, tangible and intangible, between leader and followers. A person's desire to continue to receive that flow of benefits in the future becomes a powerful incentive to accept the leadership of another person. Political leaders have traditionally used this dimension of their relations with other leaders in securing support for their actions. Certainly, many Arab leaders were willing to follow George H. W. Bush in the Gulf War to obtain or continue to receive financial and military support from the United States. And Lyndon Johnson's mastery of the Senate was due in part to his reputation of rewarding senators who supported him and punishing those who did not.

Different leaders use different methods to create a relationship with the persons they would lead. Some rely on their personal dynamism and their charisma. Other use effective strategies and techniques. Still others employ manipulation and deception. And of course, many great leaders create a relationship with their followers through their special ability to articulate compelling visions, grand designs, or glowing futures in which their followers would share.

Leaders like Winston Churchill, John F. Kennedy, and Martin Luther King created relationships with millions of people through their speeches and public appearances. Churchill successfully rallied an attacked and wounded British people to meet the Nazi threat in World War II. Kennedy, whose ringing words, "Ask not what your country can do for you; ask what you can do for your country," moved a whole generation of young Americans to commit themselves to the Peace Corps and government service. King, by declaring his dream to a million people gathered in Washington, D. C., mobilized an entire nation in the cause of civil rights. The followers of three dynamic leaders were moved to act as they did because of the relationship—the connection—that they felt with an aging British politician, a young American president, and a courageous African-American minister.

Communication as the Key to Leadership Relationships

How did these three men create that relationship? They did it through communication. Churchill, Kennedy, and King created that relationship through their extraordinary communication skills. Communication is fundamental to building relationships and therefore to the ability to lead. Indeed, leadership could not exist without communication.

Leaders communicate to their followers in many ways, but one can basically divide leadership communications into two types: mass-produced and tailor-made. Mass-produced communications, like speeches at conventions and television appearances, are designed to reach and affect large numbers of persons at one time. Tailor-made communications, like those that take place in private meetings and telephone conversations, are shaped and directed to influence specific persons.

Churchill, Kennedy, and King were virtuosos of mass-produced leadership communication—of communication from a distance. Their genius was their ability to use mass-produced leadership techniques from afar, primarily through the use of radio and television, to create relationships that millions of their followers believed were intimate and personal—relationships with "Winston," "Jack," and "Martin," persons whom they had never actually met in person but whom they did not need to meet to have a connection with.

Leadership up Close and Personal

Building relationships with other leaders for the purpose of leading them also requires effective communication. While leaders, like anyone else, can be moved by eloquent speeches, the most effective way to influence them to act for the benefit of an organization or group is to build the necessary relationship with them, not in crowds, public arenas, or the media, but one-on-one. Smart, talented, rich, and powerful people require one-on-one leadership, tailor-made leadership, leadership up close and personal.

As we saw in Chapter 1, President George H. W. Bush understood this necessity in forging a coalition for the Gulf War and so based his leadership upon his close personal relationship with other world leaders; however, his son, who did not have those relationships, did not and could not do the same when he decided to attack Iraq.

> Smart, talented, rich, and powerful people require one-on-one leadership, tailor-made leadership, leadership up close and personal.

Similarly, one of the reasons Chief Justice John Marshall was able to lead the other U.S. Supreme Court justices to unanimous opinions on key constitutional principles that laid the foundation for the American republic was the fact that he arranged for them all to live together in the same Washington board-inghouse, where they shared meals together, often over a bottle of claret provided by Marshall, and discussed their cases, the politics of the day, and life itself.[4] What Marshall did through that process was to build strong working relations with and among his colleagues, relationships that would enable him to lead the Supreme Court as one of the most effective chief justices in the history of the United States.

Despite their gifted oratory, Churchill, Kennedy, and King could not have achieved what they did without hundreds, even thousands of one-on-one meetings and conversations with other leaders—individual legislators, politicians, financial contributors, and media commentators—who had to be moved individually, one at a time, to follow these leaders in their causes. And while Lyndon Johnson, Kennedy's successor, was not a great orator, he was a master of the one-on-one encounter, a mastery that led directly to his major achievements, including his dominance and transformation of the U.S. Senate as majority leader and later, as President, the passage of Medicare and the Civil Rights Act of 1964. Leading leaders requires a one-on-one approach to leadership.

Interest-Based Leadership

A basic question that any leader should constantly ask is: Why should other people follow me? If your answer to that question is your "charisma," the exalted office you hold, or their personal loyalty to you, you are probably deluding yourself. Your charisma, your office, and their loyalty may play a role in how others relate to you, but the unvarnished answer to that fundamental question is that other persons will follow you because they judge it in their interest to do so.

Persons in groups or alone always give first priority to their own interests. Their actions are driven by their interests as they perceive them. They therefore follow their leaders when they believe that it is in their interests. Churchill, Kennedy, and King convinced their followers that the actions they were advocating would lead to a better future, a future that in one way or another and despite the costs would advance their followers' interests, whether it was to preserve British freedom, create a more dynamic America, or eliminate racism in the United States.

If you want to lead other leaders, you must focus on their individual interests. Indeed, those interests are at the heart of the challenge of leading leaders because their knowledge, talents, wealth, and connections often give them the ability to assert and defend those interests to a greater extent than many other members of an organization or group. Effective leadership lies in recognizing other leaders' interests, understanding them in all their complexity, influencing them, and then finding modes of action that will satisfy those interests while achieving desired organizational goals. Leading leaders is interest-based leadership.

To understand the interests of the leaders you lead, you must focus not only on their personal interests but also on the interests of their constituencies and followers. An overwhelming interest of most leaders is to maintain the support of their constituencies and followers; consequently, they will usually seek to avoid actions that may lose them that support—actions that they consider not in their followers' interests. So in seeking to lead other leaders, you must always try to answer the following four questions:

1. Who are their constituents and followers?
2. How important are those constituents to the leader you are seeking to lead?
3. What are those constituents' interests?
4. How will your desired course of action affect the interests of that person's constituents and followers?

It is through one-on-one encounters that leaders are best able to answer those questions and to create the relationships that address

other leaders' interests most effectively. One-on-one leadership encounters occur with many different kinds of persons in many different
contexts—with a labor leader in collective bargaining sessions, with
an investor in the board room, with an alienated executive on the
elevator. Effective leaders tailor their approach in a one-on-one meeting to the particular situation they face, and they use different communications styles in different contexts. The essence of all leadership
lies in compelling communication. Effective leaders must find the
right leadership voice for the particular one-on-one meeting at hand.

The importance of interest-based, one-on-one leadership of other
leaders is illustrated by the acquisition in July 2003 of Matador Petroleum Corporation, a privately-held oil and gas firm based in Dallas,
Texas, by Tom Brown, Incorporated, an independent petroleum company listed on the New York Stock Exchange. In 1985, Joe Foran, then
a thirty-something Texas lawyer with experience in the oil and gas
industry, established Matador Petroleum Corporation to find and develop oil and gas deposits in the American southwest. Starting in a
one-room office with a single part-time employee, Foran, through a
series of shrewd acquisitions, built Matador into one of the larger
privately-held petroleum firms in Texas. To raise capital, he brought
into the company wealthy individuals and institutional investors,
some of whom were given seats on the Matador board of directors.
With a 10 percent interest in the company, Foran, who was both
chairman and CEO, remained Matador's largest individual investor.

In the spring of 2003, Tom Brown offered to buy Matador for $388
million. Foran opposed the offer since he felt that that Matador still
had a great potential for growth that the Tom Brown offer failed to
take into account. At the board meeting to discuss the offer, Foran
was astounded to discover that the other directors were prepared to
accept it. In fact, they voted to approve the sale despite Foran's mis-
givings. Foran realized too late that he had lost the leadership of his
board. He told me, "As chairman, I thought I had been leading the
other directors in the boardroom at our quarterly meetings. I should
have been trying to lead them one-on-one outside the boardroom a

lot more frequently." A one-on-one leadership relationship with each of the directors would have enabled him to stay informed of their concerns and to prevent the formation of the coalition of directors that emerged at the meeting to accept the buy-out offer.

Foran also realized too late that he had misjudged the other directors' interests when he assumed they were the same as his own. A vigorous man in his fifties, Foran had the energy, talent, and time to build a company that would give him financial security in his retirement, still many years away. Most of the other directors were retired individual investors in their seventies who had been hurt by a falling stock market and declining returns on their investments. Their interest was not to build a company but to make an immediate profit—to take the money and run. And that was exactly what they did. Foran never found the right leadership voice to persuade the other directors that it was in their best interests to reject Tom Brown's offer. Had Foran understood those interests earlier through one-on-one meetings, he might have been able to structure a deal that gave his directors the cash they needed and allowed him to keep control of his company.

Choosing the Right Leadership Medium

In delivering any message to followers, a leader must first make a key strategic decision: How should I deliver the message? Do I make a speech or public presentation? Do I communicate one-on-one with the persons I am seeking to lead? As I have argued earlier, the most effective way of connecting to other leaders is through a one-on-one encounter.

Once a leader opts for a one-on-one exchange, it is important to realize that it can take can take place through a variety of media: a face-to-face conversation, a telephone call, a video teleconference, an e-mail exchange, a written memorandum, a letter, a hand-written note, or a fax. In undertaking a one-on-one communication, a leader must therefore make another important strategic decision: What medium should I use?

Marshall MacLuhan, the great communication theorist, is famous for his statement: "The medium is the message."[5] One may debate the validity of that statement, but in deciding on the means of communicating to other leaders you should recognize that the medium chosen *sends a message* to the persons with whom you want to communicate, in addition to the content conveyed through the medium. In short, the medium you use says things about you and about your relationship with the person you are trying to lead.

For example, if you are a company CEO seeking to persuade your board of directors to support you in making an acquisition of another firm, you could personally visit each key director to explain the acquisition's importance or you could send each of them a detailed memorandum stating the terms and consequences of the deal. A personal visit says that the individual director's support is important, that you respect that person's autonomy and judgment, and that the director plays a vital role in the organization. On the other hand, a written memorandum mailed to all directors can signal other, more negative messages, intended or unintended: that their support is taken for granted, that you place little value on their opinions, and that you, not they, are running the show.

Similarly, when George W. Bush chose to announce his actions leading up to the Iraq war through the press, without communicating personally and directly with European leaders, his choice of medium contained the message that he did not consider those leaders important to his plans and that their views in any case would have no impact on his decisions. German Chancellor Gerhard Schröder expressed his dissatisfaction with the medium when he said in an interview with the *New York Times*: "It is not good enough if I learn from the American press about a speech which

> The medium you use says things about you and about your relationship with the person you are trying to lead.

clearly states: 'We are going to do it no matter what the world and our allies think.' That is no way to treat others.'"[6] What Schröder really meant was that sending messages via the press was no way to treat other *leaders*. On the other hand, a decade earlier, when George H. W. Bush personally telephoned individual foreign leaders many times to build his coalition, the very fact of presidential telephone calls was a sign of respect and deference to those leaders and a message that their participation in the coalition was vital.

Each medium has its benefits and costs, its advantages and disadvantages. Visiting each director personally to explain the proposed merger will of course entail significant amounts of the CEO's time. On the other hand, a personal visit will enable the CEO to understand the directors' interests and positions and thus head off any possible opposition to the planned acquisition. Consulting personally with foreign leaders before acting may slow down or impede needed action. On the other hand, their ideas when given in private may be useful in making the contemplated foreign policy action more effective.

The skilled leader must evaluate these costs and benefits in making a decision on the medium to be employed. It is important, however, to be honest in your evaluation. One dean of a school at a well-regarded university had a tendency to respond to all problems raised by faculty members through a formal memorandum that was somewhat brusque in tone, a fact that only antagonized the faculty. The medium chosen by the dean sent negative messages to the faculty: that the dean was in charge and that they should obey orders; that he was too busy to spend the time to talk to them about their problems; that the dean's view of the problem was the only correct view.

When asked about his method of communicating with faculty, the dean replied that he was too busy with school fund raising, a new building program, the recruitment of new professors, and the resolution of student issues to spend time with individual faculty members on what were really small problems. Despite that explanation, persons who knew the dean well realized that he had a deep aversion to confronting conflict and that memoranda on nettlesome problems allowed him to avoid the emotional costs of a one-on-one meeting with individual professors. Ironically, his choice of communication medium served only to increase the level of conflict between him and his faculty.

The Building Blocks of Leadership Relationships

Effective communication is only the first building block necessary for an effective leadership relationship with other leaders. Three others, which will be alluded to throughout this book, are also important: commitment, reliability, and respect.

    1. *Commitment.* Good leaders clearly convey to their followers that they are working to help them and to advance their interests. Commitment, however, is more than a mere declaration by a leader to followers that "I am on your side." Followers will judge whether a leader has a genuine commitment on the basis of the leader's behavior over the course of the relationship. For example, by going to jail and by risking his life in marches and demonstrations, Martin Luther King clearly demonstrated his commitment to civil rights and to the interests of millions of African-Americans. On the other hand, corporate leaders who declare their "commitment" to employees in a speech one day and the next engage in massive layoffs have little credibility as leaders committed to their followers.

    2. *Reliability.* For any leader, an important tool of leadership is the promise, a statement of intended future action. Leaders are constantly making promises to their followers—to lower taxes, to prevent terrorist attacks, to improve profitability. Reliability in a leadership relationship means essentially that a leader keeps his promises and commitments to other persons. Once followers start to doubt a leader's reliability, the leadership relationship will begin to erode and with it a leader's ability to lead. Reliability also implies honesty. As many politicians like President Richard Nixon and countless corporate exec-

utives like WorldCom's CEO Bernard Ebbers have discovered, one of the quickest ways to lose your power to lead is to be caught committing acts that are illegal, immoral, or unethical.

3. *Respect.* Effective leadership relations require leaders to have respect for their followers as persons. This is particularly true in leading elite followers—smart, talented, rich, and powerful people. As a leader, you have to respect them and demonstrate that respect to them if you expect them to follow you. President George H. W. Bush's evident respect for the leaders of other nations facilitated his development of effective working relations with them in building a coalition to drive Iraq from Kuwait in 1991. On the other hand, many European leaders, like Germany's Gerhardt Schröder, interpreted George W. Bush's actions leading up to the invasion of Iraq as a lack of respect for them as persons and as leaders, and this factor clearly inhibited the development of leadership relations.

Conclusion: Rules for Building Relationships

Your ability to lead other leaders—to cause smart, talented, rich and powerful people to follow you—depends on the nature of the relationship that you have built with them. Building those relationships requires:

1. One-on-one interactions with them
2. An understanding of their interests
3. Effective communication of your commitment, reliability, and respect in satisfying those interests

Leadership relations are dynamic. They are capable of changing for the better or for worse. Once you have developed positive relationships with the persons you lead, you then have to work hard to nurture them. All relations are born, grow, change, and sometimes die as a result of one-on-one interactions between the persons concerned.

For the most part, those interactions are quite simply conversations. In the next chapter we will look at the role of conversation in leading leaders.

Notes

1. For brief histories of leadership scholarship, see Deanne den Hartog, "A Serious Topic for the Social Sciences," *European Business Forum* (Summer 2003), p. 7; and Robert Goffee and Gareth Jones, "Why Should Anyone Be Led By You?" *Harvard Business Review* (September-October 2000), pp. 63, 64.

2. James MacGregor Burns, *Leadership* (New York: HarperCollins, 1978).

3. William A. Welsh, *Leaders and Elites* (New York: Holt Rinehart and Winston, 1979).

4. Jean Edward Smith, *John Marshall: Definer of a Nation* (New York: Henry Holt, 1996), pp. 286-287.

5. Marshall McLuhan, *Understanding Media: The Extensions of Man* (New York: McGraw-Hill, 1964).

6. Quoted in Philip H. Gordon and Jeremy Shapiro, *Allies at War: America, Europe, and the Crisis Over Iraq* (New York: McGraw-Hill, 2004), p. 100.

THE ART OF STRATEGIC LEADERSHIP CONVERSATION

Surely, whoever speaks to me in the right voice, him or her I shall follow.

—WALT WHITMAN

THE GREAT AMERICAN POET Walt Whitman understood that persuasive communication—what he called "the right voice"—is fundamental to effective leadership. In stressing that a potential leader had to speak to *him* (and not just to the world at large) in the right voice, Whitman also underscored the importance of shaping leadership communications to meet the concerns, interests, and styles of the particular persons that a leader wants to lead.

The Game of Strategic Conversation

Much of the work of leading leaders takes place in conversations. Conversations of course have many purposes and functions. The aim of many conversations is merely to exchange information. Others, like chats around the water cooler about last night's television program, entertain, amuse, or just pass the time. But the conversations that leaders engage in with other leaders are special. They are *strategic* con-

versations. They are strategic because their purpose is to achieve the
leader's goal of changing the behavior or attitudes of other leaders in
desired ways. Their purpose is to lead.

Over fifty years ago, John von Neumann and Oskar Morgenstern,
in their seminal work, *Theory of Games and Economic Behavior,* laid the
theoretical foundations of strategy when they developed what came to
be known as "game theory," a body of learning that seeks to explain
competitive situations whose outcomes depend not only on one's own
choices but also on the choices made by other persons.[1] Their work
has had profound implications for understanding a variety of activities, from auctions to zoning regulation. It is also useful for understanding and conducting strategic conversations.

Like games, strategic conversations are competitive in the sense
that each person is seeking to advance his or her interests and that
doing so requires some desired action by the other party to the conversation. Moreover, the outcome of the conversation depends not only
on the choices made by the leader but also on the choices made by the
other person. As a result, participants in a strategic conversation must
take account of and anticipate those probable choices. The leader,
alone, is unable to determine a strategic conversation's outcome. A
problem in conversations, as in games, is that you can never know
other parties' goals, intentions, and interests as well as you know your
own. You must therefore infer them from circumstantial evidence. So
a key skill for any leader is the ability to elicit as much relevant information as possible in conducting a one-on-one encounter and to interpret that information accurately.

Unlike speeches, public presentations, and other forms of mass-
produced leadership communications, which are essentially one-way
messages from leader to followers, strategic conversations are interactive, two-way communications. While the leader is communicating a
message to influence a potential follower's behavior, the follower is at
the same time also sending messages in hopes of influencing the
leader. To use a sports analogy: Whereas speeches are a lot like playing
golf—since your score for a round depends almost entirely on your

own strokes—strategic conversations are more like tennis, since your score in the match depends on both your own and your opponent's shots. In game theory terminology, an individual orator controls the "variables" that affect results to a greater extent than does an individual in a strategic conversation who must also be concerned about the variables affecting other participants' behaviors.

For several years, I have taught an executive training program on leadership communication. At the beginning of each session, I always ask participants which forms of leadership communication—speeches or one-on-one conversations—they find more difficult. Invariably, a majority in each program claims that speeches and public presentations are more difficult. While that response may seem natural because of the tensions and emotions that giving a speech often creates in a speaker, from an analytical point of view that reaction is curious because one-on-one strategic conversations are much more complex than giving a speech.

> Elicit as much relevant information as possible in conducting a one-on-one encounter and strive to interpret that information accurately.

Unlike speeches, one-on-one leadership conversations are:

1. *Interactive,* so you have to be concerned not only about the message you are giving, but also about the messages you are receiving from other participants.

2. *Conflicted,* since they often involve conflicts, usually arising from differing interests, between the leader and others involved in the conversation.

3. *Personal,* since they usually concern the personal feelings and thoughts of the participants.

4. *Individualized,* since the conversation is tailored to the personalities and interests of the particular persons involved.

While a leader may deliver the same speech on many occasions to different audiences, each one-on-one strategic conversation is unique.

Each is tailor-made for the situation and the persons involved. A CEO of a manufacturing company will often make the same successful motivational talk to the company's distributors at several regional meetings around the country, but will need to conduct individualized strategic conversations with each company vice president to secure their buy-in on restructuring plans having a negative impact on their budgets.

Strategic leadership conversations arise in a variety of circumstances and take many forms. Some are planned well in advance; others are spontaneous. Some are cordial; others are highly conflicted. Some are emotional; others are matter-of-fact. In view of their diversity, how best can leaders conduct strategic conversations to achieve their objectives? What principles should they follow to make their strategic conversations with other leaders as effective as possible? This chapter explains the seven basic principles of the art of strategic leadership conversations. To illustrate them in a concrete way, we begin with a case that unexpectedly confronts a leader with the need to conduct a strategic conversation with a key associate.

The Case of Hans Brandt

You are the leader of a software development team that has been successful in creating new products. You believe that your team's success has been due to your efforts to develop a sense of cohesion and teamwork among your team members, a dynamic group of software engineers in their twenties and thirties. An important aspect of your leadership approach is holding staff meetings twice a week, at 9 A.M. on Monday and Thursday, for team members to share ideas and resolve problems.

Six months ago, your company acquired the U.S. subsidiary of a German software manufacturer. As part of the integration the two companies, Hans Brandt, a German software engineer in his late fifties, was assigned to your team. Although Brandt attends staff meetings irregularly and says little or nothing when he does attend, he is technically brilliant and his work is excellent. More important, he has recently proposed an innovative project idea that your company's executive committee has just agreed to fund.

When you tell Hans of the company's decision during a conversation in your office, Hans thanks you for your support and assures you of his complete dedication to the project. As he is about to leave you office, he says: "By the way, I have decided not go to staff meetings any more. Staff meetings just waste my time. People talk but they have nothing to say. They are all very young. In my old company, we never had so many meetings. Please excuse me. I have to get back to work." He rises to leave your office. As leader of the software development team, how will you respond?[2]

Seven Principles of Strategic Leadership Conversations

Despite their individualized, personal nature, one-on-one strategic conversations are subject to certain rules and principles that facilitate the task of leading other leaders. These rules recognize that leading leaders is an interest-based process, a process that assumes that the relationship between a leader and the persons to be led is a constant, interactive dynamic and that causing persons in an organization to act in desired ways for the benefit of the group requires: one, an understanding of those persons' interests, and two, techniques to shape those interests in ways that will encourage desired action.

1. Define and Stay Focused on Your Goal

Before you begin a strategic conversation, you should form a clear vision of what you want to accomplish in the meeting and keep that goal firmly in mind throughout. What is it that you want to achieve with Hans? You may decide that his new project is important and justifies his missing staff meetings, to which he was contributing little anyway. That decision lets you avoid a conflict with Hans. You also avoid the need for a strategic conversation on the subject.

On the other hand, after considering what is best for your team as well as for your own leadership, you may decide that your goal is to convince Hans to attend staff meetings regularly and contribute to them productively. Don't forget, as an experienced software engineer, Hans has valuable knowledge to share with your team, many of whom are just beginning their careers. Your team also needs to stay aware of and contribute to the development of Hans's new project, and his regular attendance at staff meetings is an important way of achieving that objective. After all, Hans is new to the company and doesn't fully know the range of its resources that can help him. And finally, allowing him to miss staff meetings may encourage other team members to do the same thing and thus destroy the team cohesion that you have worked so carefully to develop.

After considering all of these factors, you decide that your goal with Hans is to convince him to attend staff meetings and to participate in them in a constructive way. While you as leader might simply order Hans to attend meetings, that approach is likely to lead to mere passive attendance and his growing resentment toward you and other team members, persons whom he does not seem to respect much any way. To achieve your goal, you will need to engage in a strategic conversation with Hans, a conversation that hopefully in the end will allow you to change Hans's behavior for the benefit of the organization.

In an interactive conversation, unlike a prepared speech, it is easy to lose sight of your goal, particularly if the other person is working hard to deflect you from your objective, a common technique by those who seek to resist another person's leadership. So for example, if you are the president of a nonprofit organization and are meeting with one of your wealthy trustees to ask for a major gift, you may find that a reluctant trustee will use various tactics to steer the conversation toward other subjects and away from any opportunity for fund raising. One tactic is for the trustee to ask your advice on "a matter of great concern," causing you to become so engrossed in responding to the request for advice that you lose track of time and find that the half hour granted you is at an end before you have had a chance ask for the gift. Rather than merely hoping that an opportunity will arise to ask for the gift or vainly trying to steer the conversation stealthily toward the subject you want to discuss, a better approach is to make the purpose your meeting clear to the other person at the outset of your strategic conversation.

2. Get to Know the Other Person and Particularly That Person's Interests

All persons, but especially those who are leaders themselves, want and need to be treated as distinct individuals, not just one in a crowd of followers. So, if you want to lead them, you need to focus on and understand them as individuals. You must avoid the tendency to see them as your "troops," your "team," your "organization"—a faceless group of people who are pretty much the same and who are fairly interchangeable. Because of their brains, talents, wealth, and power, they are not the same. They are not interchangeable. There is only one Hans Brandt.

As you think about your problem with Hans Brandt, you should ask yourself how well you know him. If you conclude that you don't know him well, you need to find a way to get to know him. If you are the managing partner of a law firm, the director of a consulting company, or the administrator of a hospital, each of the lawyers, management consultants, or doctors that you lead is a unique individual who requires a tailor-made relationship with you if you are to lead them effectively. In order to build that relationship, you need to spend time and effort to get to know them. To come to know

> Avoid the tendency to dominate conversations and to talk more than listen, a tendency that has the effect of inhibiting the persons you are trying to lead.

others, you should follow three basic rules: a. Listen, b. Ask, and c.
Let them know you.

Listen

When we think of great leaders, we usually think first of their oratori-
cal powers and skills. No less important than their ability to talk is
their ability to listen. Unfortunately, while leaders believe they are
listening to their followers, they too often have a tendency, because of
their position, to dominate conversations and to talk more than listen,
a tendency that has the effect of inhibiting the persons they are trying
to lead. Leaders often talk more than listen, because truly listening is
a lot harder than talking.

One of Lyndon Johnson's great gifts as a leader, a gift that enabled
him to dominate the U.S. Senate, was his ability to "read men," to
come to know them, to understand their needs, their ambitions, and
their fears. To do that, of course, he had to listen. In his biography of
Johnson, Robert Caro graphically describes Johnson's concentration
and power as a listener, an indispensable tool that he used skillfully
to become the unquestioned leader of the U.S. Senate in his day and
certainly the most powerful majority leader of the twentieth century.
Describing Johnson on the telephone with another senator whose
support he sought, Caro writes:

> The hand gripping the telephone would not move, the
> eyes next to the telephone, narrowed to unblinking slits,
> gleamed black with concentration. . . . Lyndon Johnson
> would stand or sit that way for a long time, motionless,
> intent, listening—pouring himself into that listening, all
> his being focused on what the other man was saying,
> and what the man wasn't saying: on what he knew
> about the other man and on what he didn't know and
> was trying to find out.[3]

In seeking to lead other leaders, you can do no less. You must pour
yourself into listening in order to grasp and decipher the many mes-

sages that other person's seemingly simple statements contain. As leader of the software development team, you must pour yourself into listening to Hans Brandt. If you reflect back on Hans's brief communication to you as he was leaving your office, you will realize that a single communication often contains many messages and that Hans, when he told you he did not intend to come to staff meetings any longer, was also saying other things:

> "I'm learning nothing at staff meetings."
>
> "My status as a senior engineer is neither recognized nor appreciated."
>
> "I have much more experience and knowledge than the others."
>
> "Your team members are inexperienced and talk too much."
>
> "It's better to spend time working on projects than sitting uselessly at meetings."

Hans may even be saying, "Because of the way you run your team and your insistence on useless, time-consuming meetings, I don't think that you are a very effective leader."

As you think about your problem with Hans, you will probably conclude that you need to know him better if you are to find a way through strategic conversation to achieve your goal. The primary source of that information is Hans himself, and you need to find a way to persuade him to share it with you.

One of the reasons that some people find it hard to listen is that their minds process information much faster than others can speak. As a result, their underutilized brain starts searching for other things to do, such as talking or thinking about other things. In order to help you focus on listening in strategic conversations, you might develop the habit of taking notes as the other person talks. Note taking not only helps you concentrate on listening, it will also give you a record of what is said and signal to other persons in the conversation that you are taking them seriously.

Ask

One way to get to know Hans better is to ask him about himself and his background. That does not mean that you should conduct what amounts to a police interrogation, something that would cause him to become cautious and reserved. Indeed, questions from a leader to a follower can be interpreted as criticism or challenges so you need to be careful how you phrase and deliver them. Recall that Lawrence Summers, the president of Harvard, gained a reputation for bullying the smart and talented people in his university because what he considered his "provocative questions intended to generate debate" were interpreted by many members of the Harvard faculty as insulting and intended to stifle discussion.

One approach for getting to know the other person is to develop your questions naturally and neutrally from what that person has told you. For example, picking up on Hans Brandt's reference to his "old company," you might ask him how software development teams were led and managed in his old company, an avenue of discussion that will give you important information about Hans's background and his interests.

Persons in leadership position often seem strangely reluctant to ask questions of the persons they lead. Perhaps they think that questioning is a sign of ignorance and therefore will cast a negative reflection on their leadership. After all, doesn't a strong leader have all the answers, while a weak leader doesn't know what to do? Some leaders may fear that asking questions may be seen as evidence that they don't know what to do.

On the other hand, perhaps their reluctance to ask questions reflects a fear that they will receive information they don't want to hear, information that contains negative judgments on the quality of their leadership. The question, however, is a very powerful leadership tool, a tool that enables you not only to solve problems but equally important to get to know the people you want to lead. The question is not only a means to gain information, but it also serves to communicate with the other person. For one thing, through your questioning you can communicate that the other person is important to you, that you care about that person's concerns, ideas and feelings. In short, asking questions, if done right, can acknowledge the other person's status as a leader.

Your purpose in getting to know the persons you lead is especially to understand their interests, since it is those interests that drive their actions, actions you need to influence for the benefit the organization or group that you lead. Getting to know the interests of another person can be a very complex, time-consuming process. It is complicated by various factors.

First, the persons you lead may not want to tell you their interests in detail for fear of causing you to draw negative implications. For example, a research molecular biologist in your organization may be reluctant to tell you that her status and reputation among other research scientists working in the same field around the world counts much more for her than her status in your organization, your judgment of her, or even your organization's financial results in the next quarter.

Second, a person usually has many different interests, some more important than others. Thus, a challenge for a leader is not only to determine those interests but to understand their differing priorities.

Third, the process of determining interests is complicated by the fact that people have a tendency to state their positions toward a particular event, policy, or proposed plan of action, rather than to explain the interests that led them to that position. For example, the molecular biologist may flatly state that she is against undertaking a new research project for various technical reasons, rather than articulate her underlying fear that it will take her to an area of research that her professional colleagues do not hold in high regard and that as a result her own reputation as a scientist will suffer.

> Use questions to probe the underlying interests of the persons you hope to lead.

As a leader, you should use questions to probe the underlying interests of the persons you hope to lead. So in your conversation with Hans Brandt, you need to determine the interests that are driving his actions and attitudes in your organization. After some discussions, you may realize that Hans has several interests: recognition by the organization of his status as a senior engineer; success in developing his new project; and a desire to undertake other new projects in the future, among others.

Finally, the process of determining interests may be complicated by the leader's premature assumptions about the other person's interests, assumptions that have no basis in fact. Just as Joe Foran wrongly assumed that his and his directors' financial interests in Matador Petroleum were identical, the CEO of a company employing the molecular biologist might wrongly assume that her primary interest is the money she earns from the company. Thus he may proceed to develop financial incentives to induce desired action from her, when in fact her professional standing in the scientific community is the interest that primarily drives her actions.

Failure to understand the complexity of interests of other leaders may have contributed to General Electric's inability to secure approval from the European Union competition authorities of its acquisition of Honeywell in 2001. Considering approval a "done deal," GE executives showed little deference to European officials. Early in the discussions, in what was obviously an attempt at one-on-one relationship building, Jack Welch, GE's legendary CEO, said to Mario Monti, the European Union's competition commissioner, as if they were in a private business negotiation, "Call me Jack." Monti, keenly aware that he represented the European public interest, replied: "I'll only call you Jack when this deal is over." The talks went downhill from there.[4]

While the head of GE might have been correct in assuming that other corporate executives would have an interest in being on a first-name basis with Jack Welch, perhaps in hopes of developing a relationship that would lead to future business, he erred if he thought that a high ranking foreign government official seeking to assert his government's and his own dignity would have the same interest. Monti's and the E.U.'s interests were deference to their authority, not friendship.

Let Them Know You

Often, in order to get to know other leaders and to build a necessary connection for leadership, you need to let them know you. While a one-on-one encounter should never be dominated by an exposition of your achievements and opinions, the judicious interjection of information about yourself can help to develop a relationship with other persons, a relationship that will make them feel enough trust in you to allow them to reveal important information about their interests and goals.

In his memoir, *Turmoil and Triumph*, former U. S. Secretary of State George Shultz gives a graphic example of how a Russian counterpart at the 1986 Reykjavik Summit between President Ronald Reagan and President Mikhail Gorbachev provided information about himself that led to the development of an effective working relationship between the two sides. In an early meeting with Shultz, Marshal Sergei Akhromeyev, then deputy minister of defense, remarked that he was "one of the last of the Mohegans [sic]," meaning that he was the last of the Soviet World War II commanders still in service. When Shultz asked Akhromeyev where he learned the expression "last of the Mohegans [sic]," Akhromeyev replied that he had been raised on the novels of the American writer James Fenimore Cooper. The answer had an immediate impact on Shultz. It led him to conclude that Akhromeyev was more open and ready for conversation than previous Soviet negotiators, that he was a man with a sense of history and an awareness of the American way, and that he was a person the Americans could deal with. "Literature can build bridges," Shultz wrote.[5] As a result, Akhromeyev became Shultz's primary conduit of communication to the Russian side throughout the entire summit.

3. Appeal to and Shape Those Interests

Once you understand the interests of the persons you would lead, you need to appeal to and shape them in a way that will bring about desired behavior. Sometimes leaders try to induce their followers to give up their interests for the sake of "the company," "the organization," or even for the leader personally. These types of appeals are not likely to bring about desired results or may require undesirable forms of coercion—especially with persons who are themselves leaders.

So while ordering Hans to attend staff meetings may result in his physically being present, it is hardly likely to achieve the result you want, which is his productive engagement in meeting discussions. Ordinarily, people will not substitute their own interests for the greater good of the company, the organization, or even the country unless they are convinced that their interests and the company's, organization's, or country's are similar and that the organization, company, or country will enable them to achieve interests that they could not achieve alone.

At the same time, effective leaders know how to shape and interpret the interests of their followers to align them with leadership goals. They use a variety of techniques to achieve this end. Among the more common techniques are the following:

Framing

Framing is a process of characterizing or explaining a situation in a particular way. Leaders seek to mobilize their followers to take action by characterizing a problem or challenge in such away that it is in their interests to do something about it. So in building a coalition to drive Iraq out of Kuwait in 1991, President George H. W. Bush could have framed the problem of Iraq's occupation of Kuwait in a variety of ways: as a threat to western oil supplies, as the need to protect the people of a friendly country, or as the necessity of stopping a brutal dictator. While he may have suggested these factors at various times, to convince other leaders to join the coalition, he consistently framed the Iraq invasion as a fundamental threat to the

> Move your followers to take action by characterizing a problem or challenge in such away that it is in their interests to do something about it.

common interests of all countries in preserving the territorial integrity of states, of preserving the international rule of law and the principles of the U.N. Charter, and of the international system itself. Countries, large and small, understood that rolling back Iraq's occupation of Kuwait was in their interests. Because that common interest was so clear, it was easy for national leaders to convince their citizens that participation in the coalition was in their countries' interests.

By contrast, George W. Bush's method of framing the need to go to war in Iraq in 2003 had quite the opposite effect because it failed to accommodate the interests of many other nations. His decision to frame the conflict with Iraq as a struggle of good against evil and as the right of America to take preemptive action any time it sensed a threat changed the debate among other national leaders from what to do about Iraq to the new role of the United States in the international order.[6] On the other hand, in seeking to gain domestic American support for the invasion of Iraq, President Bush, after advancing other justifications, ultimately came to frame military action as part of the war on terrorism, knowing of Americans' overriding interest in security from terrorism as a result of the attacks against the World Trade Center on September 11, 2001.

Bargaining

A second important means of influencing other leaders is through *quid pro quo* bargaining. By this technique, a leader seeks to secure desired action from followers in return for some action by the leader in the follower's interest. Political leaders from time immemorial have secured the loyalty of their followers through promises of "patronage"—jobs, contracts, and favors that the leader is able to grant. Leaders of private sector and nonprofit organizations, while not using the term "patronage," nonetheless dispense special favors in return for the support of the persons whom they lead in those organizations. Sometimes the bargain for the favor is explicit; sometimes it is implicit. For example, the CEO of a corporation might promise an executive who is key to securing a change in the company's business strategy an increase in salary and elevation to executive vice president.

If Hans's interest is having his status recognized within the organization, you may have to strike a bargain with him that he will attend staff meetings to keep the others aware of his exciting new project and that in return he will be given a special role, as a senior engineer, in those meetings.

Bargains struck with followers can sometimes cause problems later on for a leader. For one thing, others in the organization who do not benefit from them may become disgruntled because they believe the leader is playing favorites, an accusation that may ultimately undermine a leader's legitimacy. For another, some bargains, which may seem at first glance to be purely an internal matter, may violate the law or have unforeseen consequences for the organization's other relationships.

In 2000, Sanford Weill, the dynamic chairman and CEO of Citigroup, the world's largest financial services company, sought to persuade Jack Grubman, one of the corporation's top research analysts, to give a favorable rating to AT&T so that Citigroup might have an improved chance of obtaining substantial investment banking business from the telecommunications giant. In return, Weill promised to help Grubman's children gain admission to one of New York City's exclusive private schools. Judging this bargain to be unlawful interference in the research process and ultimately the functioning of the market, the New York attorney general brought charges against both Citigroup and Weill. Ultimately, the matter required a settlement of several hundred million dollars.

Mobilizing Social Pressure by Third Parties

Too often, leaders wrongfully believe that the leadership of an organization depends only on their skills, and their skills alone. Leaders' resources include not only their personal talents, but the web of relationships they have with other persons. So a third important technique for securing desired action by followers, particularly if they are also leaders, is through the use of social pressure and influence on a follower by some third party at the instance of the leader. Leaders, like the rest of us, are more inclined to listen to some persons than to others and to be influenced by certain individuals rather than others.

In seeking to lead other leaders, you should try to identify third persons who have some influence over those leaders and then seek to mobilize them in your cause. For example, while in the Senate, Lyndon Johnson, a Texan, used Hubert Humphrey, a liberal from Minnesota with whom he had developed a strong working relationship, to reach out to northern Democratic liberals who did not have great trust in Johnson.[7] Similarly, in building support for a proposed acquisition, a CEO might use directors with whom he has a close relationship to influence more skeptical board members.

In one case, Reebok, the internationally known manufacturer of athletic footwear and clothing, wanted to begin talks with one of its distributors to renegotiate an existing contract to reduce the amount of its local advertising commitments. When the distributor refused such a change, Reebok asked the president of a noncompeting manufacturer, whose products were also handled by the distributor, to intervene to help settle the matter. That president had an interest in seeing the dispute settled because he feared that a protracted conflict with Reebok would weaken the distributor and thereby make the distributor less effective in handling the president's own brands. He therefore held a series of conversations with the distributor that ultimately led to a satisfactory settlement of the dispute with Reebok.[8]

To solve your problem with Hans, you may have to engage other team members in the process of integrating him more closely into the team. Hans's status as an outsider may be attributable as much to the exclusionary behavior of other team members as to the actions and attitudes of Hans himself.

4. Anticipate the Possible Actions of the Other Person

War is one of the highest exercises in strategy. It has been said that one of the most common strategic errors in warfare is to fail to take account of what the enemy may do.[9] An equally serious mistake in a strategic conversation is not to consider the various actions other persons might take in reaction to your effort to lead them. Rarely do followers docilely accept the directions of their leaders. Rarely will your charisma, oratory, and commanding presence cause them to lose sight of their interests. As we have already indicated, all followers, but especially followers who are also leaders, have their own interests and will adopt strategies and tactics to deal with their leaders in ways that will not injure those interests. So in conducting any strategic conversation, a leader must ask three questions:

1. How will my statements be interpreted by the persons I am trying to lead in light of their interests?
2. What strategies, tactics, and reactions will they take in response to my statements?
3. What should I then be prepared to do in response to their reactions?

In their book, *Thinking Strategically*, Avinash Dixit and Barry Nalebuff state that Rule No. 1 of strategic behavior is "Look ahead and reason back."[10] As the authors advise, you should anticipate where your actions will lead and use that information in making decisions on how to deal with strategic problems. For example, if your immediate response is to reject Hans's decision and instead order him to attend meetings, you should recognize that he will probably continue to attend irregularly, will certainly not participate in discussions, may embark on a strategy of passive resistance to you, and will strongly resent you and your entire team. In short, his passive attendance at meetings will not contribute much to your organization's development and indeed may harm the important project that Hans is working on.

A basic technique for anticipating the reaction of others is to put yourself in their shoes, to examine your statements and actions from their point of view and then, from that point of view, anticipate what they will say and do. If you do that and think hard about it, you will come to realize that the other person has lots of options in dealing with you and your efforts to lead them in a certain direction. Lyndon Johnson, who as Majority Leader of the Senate governed that body by leading its members one-on-one, actually rehearsed his strategic conversations out loud with other senators beforehand. Behind the closed door of his office, his aides would hear Johnson "playing out a conversation: what he would say; what the other senator would say in response; what *he* should then say. . . ."[11]

In conducting strategic conversations, we have to make assumptions. Although we know our own intentions, we can never know for sure the intentions of the person with whom we are talking. Similarly, although we know the impact of other's statements on us, we can never know with certainty the impact that we are making on others. So we are forced to make assumptions about the *intentions* of others and about our *impact* on others.[12]

For example, in conducting a strategic conversation to gain the support of one of your vice presidents for a company reorganization that will entail significant personnel changes in his division, you receive nods as you speak and receive no objections. As a result, you believe that you have convinced him to participate in the process. You are of course making an assumption about his intentions and the impact of your statement on him. While he may indeed be convinced by your logic, he may also have concluded that arguing with you is pointless and that he knows of other ways to minimize the effect of your restructuring plans on his division. Your evaluation may reflect your self-interest rather than a hard-headed appraisal of the signals you are receiving from him about his intentions. The point is that we should recognize the assumptions we make, be open to receiving signals that challenge those assumptions, test the assumptions continually, and be ready to change assumptions when the evidence warrants.

5. Generate Options Together

In conducting a strategic conversation to achieve a desired goal, an important approach is to engage the other person in a process of generating options that will allow you to achieve your objectives and at the same time satisfy some or all of that person's interests. To do that, you should try to create a climate in which the persons you are seeking to lead actually participate in the process of decision making. You invite that participation through such questions as: "What if . . . ? What about . . . ? What would it take . . . ? How have others solved this problem?" Instead of an adversary, your follower through this process will hopefully become your collaborator in solving a common problem.

Some leaders are tempted to see the option generation process as merely a formality to secure agreement by their followers. To view it in these terms is a mistake. It is an opportunity for you as a leader to learn, an opportunity to tap the knowledge and experience of your followers, who are often more expert in areas than you are. You should be ready to learn from the process and to gather ideas that will improve the eventual path on which you lead others.

In using this approach, however, you have to be aware that your followers, in generating options, may limit options suggested to those that favor their interests only or otherwise structure the option generating conversation to arrive at a desired result. For example, several years ago in seeking to resolve a conflict between a university's provost on the one hand and the deans of its schools on the other, a university president asked one of the deans what could be done. The dean replied, "It seems to me you have two options: you can either fire your provost or fire six deans." The president fired the provost. The two options suggested by the dean were not the only options, of course. The president would have been well advised to press the dean to come up with other options and to have suggested his own options to test them with the dean with whom he was having a strategic conversation, rather than let the dean control the option setting process.

> The option generation process is an opportunity for you as a leader to tap the knowledge and experience of your followers.

In addition to simply enumerating options, the way you character-ize them can have an impact on the conversation. During the Vietnam War, advisors and friends of Lyndon Johnson kept assuring him of his popularity in the United States, despite widespread public protests against him. As the 1968 presidential election approached, they all urged him to seek reelection. One advisor, however, injected a note of hard reality into the discussions when he said: "You can run, Mr. President, and you will almost certainly win. But the only places you will be able to campaign are Ft. Bragg and the aircraft carrier *Enter-prise.*" Ultimately, Johnson chose not to run.

6. Evaluate the Options Using a Fair Process

Research indicates that persons are more willing to accept an adverse decision if they believe it was arrived at through a fair process, rather than one that is arbitrary. An initial element of a fair process is that it allows followers to be heard, permits their participation, and consid-ers their interests and concerns. In many organizations, the leadership often sees objections from persons led as an annoyance at best or rank disloyalty at worst. Consequently, such leaders often ignore objec-tions, belittle them, or even ostracize persons who raise them.

President George W. Bush dealt with French and German objec-tions over his plans to go war with Iraq in this way. The Bush adminis-tration came to view both countries as disloyal and ungrateful allies and did its best to belittle their concerns publicly and to isolate them diplomatically. This approach did not cause them to fall into line. As a leadership method it failed.

As a leader of smart, talented, rich, and powerful people, you need to address their concerns, rather than belittle them, and to involve them in making leadership decisions. Another important element in a fair process is to review together the possible options for action and then evaluate their costs and benefits against some agreed upon stan-dard. So in your discussion with Hans Brandt, you might examine the various possibilities for his participation and nonparticipation in staff

meetings and their impact on team operations, on company productivity, and on his own work. If the standard of productivity is one that
you may both be able to agree on as appropriate, you may be able to
convince him that his complete absence from staff meetings may have
a negative effect on both the team's and his productivity over the long
term.

7. Decide and Gain Commitment for the Decision

Your goal in a strategic conversation is not merely to gain agreement
from persons you lead, but more important, to gain their genuine
commitment to act for the benefit of the organization in the way you
have indicated. The danger is that, having engaged in an intense strategic conversation to secure action toward an organizational goal,
whether it is restructuring of the firm, undertaking of a new line of
research, or developing an innovative financial product, the persons
you are leading might leave the meeting and do nothing to further
your goal, or worse yet, take action that sabotages any movement in a
desired direction. In former times, kings and princes gained commitment by having their followers sign a document in blood, swear on a
bible, or give their first sons as hostages. Modern managers and leaders can't use these quaint but often effective techniques today to assure commitment to an agreed course of action, but they do have
other methods at their disposal. Here are a few of them:

1. *Public Statement of Commitment.* One technique is to induce your
followers to make some sort of a statement of commitment in the
presence of others about their intended course of action. Social pressure as a result of such public statements, as well as concerns for their
own reputations, have a tendency to cause those committed to act as
they said they would. In making a decision to invade Afghanistan at a
Cabinet meeting after September 11, 2001, President George W. Bush
went around the table and asked each Cabinet member individually
whether he or she had reservations about the intended invasion.[13]

This process had the effect of causing each member of the cabinet to take ownership of this key policy decision.

2. *Installment Payments.* A second method to secure commitment is to structure the benefits that the leader is to provide the follower in installments, contingent on the follower actually performing the commitment he agreed to make. So you might make it clear to Hans that your continued support of his project with the company's executive committee will depend on his active participation in staff meetings.

3. *Agreed-Upon Verification.* In order to secure commitment and implementation of your agreement with another leader, the two of you might agree on a plan for verifying your and the other person's action. The obligation to make periodic reports or to allow you to make periodic inspections acts as a force to encourage desired action by those whom you would lead.

Conclusion: Rules for Conducting Strategic Conversations

Leading other leaders is one-on-one leadership. It requires engaging leaders on a personal basis in strategic conversations in order to understand and help to satisfy their interests so that you may satisfy your own. An effective strategic conversation requires you to:

1. Define and stay focused on your goal.
2. Get to know the other person and particularly that person's interests.
3. Appeal to and shape those interests.
4. Anticipate the possible actions of the other person.
5. Generate options together.
6. Evaluate the options using a fair process.
7. Decide and gain commitment for the decision.

In the following chapters we will look at specific leadership tasks and how to apply these principles to them.

Notes

1. John von Neumann and Oskar Morgenstern, *Theory of Games and Economic Behavior* (Princeton, N.J.: Princeton University Press, 1953).

2. A video version of this case is to be found in *Hans Brandt*, written, directed, and produced by Jeswald W. Salacuse and available from the Program on Negotiation at Harvard Law School (www.pon.org).

3. Robert A. Caro, *The Years of Lyndon Johnson: Master of the Senate* (New York: Alfred A. Knopf, 2002), pp. 491–492.

4. Jack Welch with John A. Bryne, *Jack: Straight from the Gut* (New York: Warner Books, 2000), p. 366.

5. George Shultz, *Turmoil and Triumph: My Years as Secretary of State* (New York: Charles Scribner & Sons, 1993), p. 763.

6. Philip H. Gordon and Jeremy Shapiro, *Allies at War: America, Europe, and the Crisis Over Iraq* (New York: McGraw-Hill, 2004), p. 10.

7. Caro, *The Years of Lyndon Johnson*, p. 455.

8. Author's interview with a Reebok executive, November 25, 2000.

9. Carnes Lord, *The Modern Prince: What Leaders Need to Know Now* (New Haven, Conn.: Yale University Press, 2003), p. 194.

10. Avinash K. Dixit and Barry J. Nalebuff, *Thinking Strategically: The Competitive Edge in Business, Politics, and Everyday Life* (New York: W. W. Norton, 1991), p. 34.

11. Caro, *The Years of Lyndon Johnson*, p. 503.

12. On this subject, see Douglas Stone, Bruce Patton, and Sheila Heen, *Difficult Conversations: How to Discuss What Matters Most* (New York: Penguin Putnam, 1999).

13. Bob Woodward, *Bush at War* (New York: Simon & Schuster, 2002).

CHAPTER 4

THE SEVEN DAILY TASKS OF LEADERSHIP

Leadership is action, not position.
—DONALD H. MCGANNON

THE WORK OF LEADERS rarely includes actually performing the tasks that their organizations are designed to accomplish. CEOs don't actually make the products their corporations sell. University presidents rarely teach students. Hospital administrators never treat patients. And generals hardly ever "fight" the enemy, at least in the sense that the ordinary soldier understands that word. So what is it that leaders really do?

Most discussions of leadership look at the subject from the leader's perspective, from the viewpoint of persons who are supposed to provide this elusive but supposedly essential quality to organizations and institutions. So scholars of leadership tell us what leaders do and how they do it, and leaders themselves in their memoirs recount their triumphs and failures. While an understanding of leadership from the leader's perspective is undoubtedly illuminating, it is equally important to examine leadership from the follower's point of view. Indeed, the follower's perspective may even be more important since the whole purpose of leadership is to serve the organization, not the leader.

What Followers Expect and Need

It is often said that people in organizations want and need to be led.[1] But what exactly do organizations and institutions, employees and associates expect, want, and need from their leaders? When a corporate vice president says that his company needs "better leadership," what exactly does he mean? When a professor complains of her university's "poor leadership," what precisely is she concerned about? When a museum trustee calls for more "effective museum leadership," what is it that she is seeking? As consumers of leadership, what is it that all of these people feel they need but are not getting?

One way to try to answer this question is to look at the tasks and functions that followers expect of their leaders. In making a functional analysis of leadership, we can identify seven tasks that followers in all organizations expect their leaders to deliver. A review of what leaders do and are expected to do by their followers reveals that there are seven basic tasks that leaders must accomplish every day.

The first task is *direction*. Every organization, large and small, looks to its leader to articulate and establish the goals of the organization. The process of goal setting with elite followers is usually complicated, lengthy, and elaborate. Goldman Sachs needed more than a decade of discussions among it partners to decide to sell its shares to the public. Mere articulation of the vision is not enough. Leaders must also convince their followers to accept it.

Organizations not only demand that the leaders point the way but, like shepherds directing their flock, also oversee the organization's movement in that direction. Many failures of corporate governance, such as the collapse of Enron, which led to financial loss, civil suits, and even criminal charges, have been the result of failed oversight by corporate leaders. Effective performance of the task of direction includes oversight to assure that the organization avoids the legal,

> Mere articulation of the vision is not enough. You must convince your followers to accept it.

ethical, and financial traps that lie in wait for an organization that is moving forward, especially when it is moving onto terrain it has never ventured on before.

The second everyday leadership skill is *integration*. All organizations require their leaders to bring together diverse persons, each with individual wills, differing interests, and varied backgrounds, to work for the common interests of the organization. All leaders seek in varying degrees to integrate the persons they lead into a single organization, unit, or team. That task is particularly difficult in organizations composed of smart, talented, rich, and powerful people. Many elites by nature resist efforts at integration, a fact that requires innovative approaches to the process.

The third leadership challenge is *mediation*. All organizations consist of persons with different interests, a factor that invariably results in conflict among its members. Individuals in the same organization may struggle over turf, resources, responsibilities, and policies. In many organizations, leaders settle such conflicts by fiat or by imposing a decision. That approach will not often work with other leaders over whom a leader may have little authority. In disputes among elite followers, leaders must often mediate a solution almost as if they were settling a conflict among sovereign states.

Education is the fourth everyday leadership task. Leaders educate, coach, guide, and advise the people they lead. Through that process, leaders give the necessary knowledge and skills that empower the people they lead to carry out the jobs of the organization. The traditional view is that leaders give orders to get things done in organizations. In fact, many modern leaders achieve their goals through advice and counsel. Generally speaking, the more decentralized the organization and the more educated its members, the more important advice and education become as a tool of leadership. This is especially true when

Persons you lead will look to you to motivate them, encourage them, and strengthen them to do the right thing for the organization.

leading other leaders. Because of their sense of independence and position, elite followers are often loath to seek help and quick to reject attempts to educate them.

The fifth daily skill of leadership is *motivation*. Just as the city of New York looked to Mayor Rudolph Giuliani for emotional support in the aftermath of the attack on 9/11, persons in organizations look to their leaders to motivate them, encourage them, and strengthen them to do the right thing for the organization. Elites, however, are often less inclined to seek such emotional support since they fear to do so would reduce their power, influence, and elite status within the organization. Moreover, they may not respond to the traditional incentives and motivators that corporations often employ.

Representation is the sixth daily leadership task. Leaders are constantly representing the organizations they lead, whether they are negotiating a labor contract or attending a reception given by a customer, whether they are persuading their superiors to increase a departmental budget or advocating the promotion of a valued associate. Representing smart, talented, rich, and powerful people raises special challenges since they are often reluctant to grant full authority of representation to their leader and demand to ratify any and all of actions taken by that leader on their behalf with external parties. Thus, a corporate CEO negotiating the acquisition of another firm can usually operate with full authority and not be too concerned about retaining internal support throughout the negotiations. On the other hand, managing directors of organizations composed of elites, such as a law firms or consulting companies, who negotiate acquisitions of other firms must constantly assure themselves that their mandate continues and that they maintain the support of their partners through every step in the negotiation.

> Without creating trust you will find it difficult, if not impossible, to direct, integrate, mediate, educate, motivate, or represent the persons you lead.

And finally, the seventh daily skill of leadership is *trust creation* or, more specifically, earning the trust of the persons. Creating trust is a vital skill, for without it leaders will find it difficult, if not impossible, to direct, integrate, mediate, educate, motivate, or represent the persons in their organizations. In short, without trust, a leader cannot lead effectively. Creating and maintaining the trust of an organization's elites, who are often skeptical and critical by nature because of their training, raises special challenges for its leader.

The Multitasking Leader

These seven tasks, while conceptually separate, are interrelated in practice. Helping an organization find an agreed-upon direction may also facilitate its integration, since a common goal gives a sense of unity to its members. Similarly, arriving at a common sense of direction may first require a leader to engage in extensive education about the threats and opportunities that face the organization. All good leaders perform each of these tasks every day. No leader has the luxury of focusing on one to the exclusion of all others. Leaders must multitask constantly. If they don't, they may not stay leaders for long.

Few leaders do all seven tasks equally well. Some leaders perform certain of these tasks more effectively than others because of differences in natural abilities or personal preferences. An outgoing, gregarious managing partner of a consulting or law firm may spend more time on and be more effective in representing the firm to various outside constituencies than in mediating the internal conflicts among partners that are paralyzing the firm and keeping it from adopting a new strategic direction. While resolving internal conflicts should be a matter of priority at this particular moment in the history of the firm, the managing partner without the ability or the desire to engage in conflict resolution may find more satisfying, not to say easier, ways to exercise leadership by spending time out of the office working on what he considers "essential matters" of representation.

When followers complain of poor leadership, they may be referring to a leader's performance on different tasks. A corporate vice president may feel that the CEO is not giving strong leadership because he is not articulating a vision—*a direction*—that will allow the company to face the challenge of changing technology. On the other hand, a professor, complaining of a university president's poor leadership, may mean that he is not doing enough to *motivate* and support the faculty in their work. And a museum board member lamenting the ineffective leadership of the museum's executive director may really be criticizing the director's failure to *represent* the museum powerfully to the community and thus raise the funds necessary for the museum's development.

For both leaders and followers, it is therefore essential to understand the individual tasks of leadership in all their complexity so leaders may deliver this vital commodity more effectively and followers may better evaluate and use what is being delivered.

Conclusion: Leadership's Seven Daily Tasks

Any leader must face these seven tasks every day. For leaders of other leaders, they require a special approach, as the following list reveals:

1. Direction: Negotiating the vision
2. Integration: Making stars a team
3. Mediation: Settling leadership conflicts
4. Education: Teaching the educated
5. Motivation: Moving other leaders
6. Representation: Leading outside of the organization
7. Trust Creation: Capitalizing your leadership

In the next seven chapters we will look at each of these daily tasks of leadership in detail to see in particular how you may accomplish them in leading smart, talented, rich, and powerful people.

Note

1. See, for example, Robert H. Rosen with Paul Brown, *Leading People: The Eight Proven Principles for Success in Business* (New York: Penguin Books, 1996) p. 7.

Task No. 1: Direction

Negotiating the Vision

The real leader has no need to direct—he is content to point the way.
—Henry Miller [1]

Organizations are not composed of robots controlled from a command center. Organizations consist of individuals, each with separate wills and sets of interests. If all those individuals were to exercise their own wills and pursue their interests independently and without regard to others, the organization would not likely achieve the goals for which it was established in the first place. Indeed, chaos would almost certainly result. For those wills and interests to be harnessed for the benefit of the group or organization, the organization needs a sense of direction—a sense of direction that its members have accepted and agreed to work toward.

Organizations look to their leaders to help determine that sense of direction and then assure that its members move toward it. In this regard, the leader of any organization faces three fundamental, interrelated questions:

1. How do I help my organization determine that sense of direction?

2. How do I lead my organization's members as a whole to adopt that indicated direction as a goal and work to achieve it enthusiastically?

3. How do I keep the organization moving purposefully in that direction over time yet make necessary adjustments as the unexpected arises?

Direction, the first daily task of leadership, thus has three basic components: direction determination, direction commitment, and direction oversight. Let's look at each of them in turn and see how they apply to leading other leaders.

Determining the Direction, the Way, the Vision

If every organization or group needs an agreed-upon direction toward which to move in order to function effectively, one may ask a fundamental question: Where does this sense of the organization's direction come from? Books on management and leadership stress the importance of the leader's *vision* in determining an organization's direction. Leaders exert their leadership, they tell us, by giving their organizations a "strategic vision," a picture of a new and better future. Martin Luther King was a visionary leader who galvanized the civil rights movement in the United States by eloquently painting a picture of a future in which people would be judged "not by the color of their skin but by the content of their character."

In business, the creation of an effective strategy begins first with providing the company with a strategic vision,[2] and the source of that vision is inevitably top management, if not the CEO alone. Vision has become so important in contemporary thinking on leadership that the traditional noun of "vision" has become a verb. So leaders are encouraged "to vision" and to engage in "visioning."

Jack Welch's vision of General Electric (GE) as a "primary contender"—that is, number one or number two in market share in any of its businesses—is seen as a cause of that company's success, and Sandy Weill's vision for Citigroup led it to become the biggest financial services firm in the world. Indeed, it is almost an article of faith of American business that the visionary CEO—and the visionary CEO alone—is responsible for the rise or fall of the corporation's fortunes. As a result, American CEOs not only communicate their vision to the people they manage, but they also feel compelled to share their vision as widely as possible. They write books. They appear regularly on television. They are the superstars of American corporate culture.

Despite effective performance on the part of individual CEOs, America's emphasis on the role and importance of the CEO, at least to some extent, seems derived from its cultural value of individualism. Americans believe that organizational achievement is disproportionately attributable to the actions of the individual leader, rather than to the efforts of the group. From the Lone Ranger to Huckleberry Finn, American culture is filled with tales of the individual triumphant. Translating that myth to corporate culture, the CEO has become the Lone Visioner who rides in to save companies with his vision.

In countries with a more communitarian culture, such as Germany and Japan, corporate leadership tends to be more of a group effort than in the United States. This factor may explain why European CEO compensation levels, in relation to those of other executives and employees, are not as high as they are in the United States. Moreover, European and Japanese cultures, with their emphasis on community values and their large number of family companies, seem to give the European and Japanese CEO the status of a patriarch or father figure within the corporation, rather than the heroic stature that American culture accords its own CEOs. As a result, European and Japanese cultures place much less emphasis on the individual CEO's vision as an instrument of corporate management.[3]

Much of the commentary on U.S. corporate leadership seems to presuppose that without the CEO the company has no vision, that the new CEO arrives to find a visionary *tabula rasa* within the organization. That of course is not the fact. In any organization, members throughout its structure have ideas, thoughts, images, and, yes, visions of what they would like their organization to be. In organizations and groups composed of leaders—of smart, talented, rich, and powerful people—each of them is likely to have a quite distinct organizational vision. Some members of a law firm, for example, may have a vision of their organization "as a boutique operation specializing in what it has done for the last half century," while others may view its future as a "full-service global firm with offices in major capitals." Within an investment bank, some partners may have a vision for their firm as a publicly held financial services institution, while others may view its preferred future as specializing in investment banking without outside shareholders.

In addition to their diversity of views about the future, elite followers strongly hold to their visions and will not allow a leader, no matter how charismatic, to replace them easily with his or her own vision. Thus, instead of being the organization's lone visionary, a leader of other leaders is likely to find the visionary field quite crowded indeed.

> In organizations and groups composed of leaders, each of them is likely to have a quite distinct organizational vision.

Visionary Prophet or Visionary Diplomat?

None of this is to belittle the importance of a vision in determining the strategic direction of an organization or the leader's role in shaping and articulating it. It is only to underscore that in leading other leaders, you are more likely to find a situation of *competing visions* among them rather than a group of befuddled individuals who are not quite sure of what to do and are only looking for the right leader to arrive on the scene and point the way in eloquent fashion. For leaders of most organizations, and especially of smart, talented, rich, and powerful people, the challenge of determining a direction for the group lies especially in forging a single vision out of the multiplicity of visions held by its members. Instead of handing down a vision for the organization from on high like a prophet, the process of articulating a vision in such an environment is one of negotiation.

Like a skilled diplomat in an international setting, the effective leader of leaders, whether heading an investment bank, museum board, or research institute, creates a common vision for the organization by building a coalition among its members who support that vision. Leaders of other leaders need to be visionary diplomats rather than visionary prophets.

Building a coalition in support of a vision for the organization demands intense one-on-one leadership through the effective use of strategic conversation. It is an extremely labor-intensive process, requiring the leader to connect and interact with all the key players. For example, to resolve the longstanding conflict between the United Nations and the United States over the nonpayment of its UN dues, Richard Holbrooke, then U.S. Ambassador to the United Nations, met individually with representatives from nearly 150 countries and scores of senators and congressional representatives in order to forge a coalition in support of a deal that led to a reduction in the U.S. dues rate in return for payment by the United States of dues in arrears. The techniques outlined in Chapter 3 on the art of strategic conversations are precisely the tools needed by a coalition builder.

Securing Commitment to the Direction

Having determined a direction for the organization and built the necessary supporting coalition, the leader must now secure genuine commitment from the organization's members to work toward achieving the vision. It is naïve to assume that persons in the organization will be committed to its goals for the sake of loyalty. Smart, talented, rich, and powerful people are committed to visions primarily because they perceive it is in their interests, and secondarily because of the rewarding relationships they may have with others in the organization, including the leader.

In this regard, leaders should recall the warning of Niccolò Machiavelli, still one of the world's foremost leadership thinkers, about the challenges of establishing new directions:

> And let it be noted that there is no more delicate matter to take in hand, nor more dangerous to conduct, nor more doubtful of success, than to set up as a leader in the introduction of changes. For he who innovates will have for his enemies all those who are well off under the existing order of things, and only lukewarm supporters in those who might be better off under the new.[4]

Modern psychological research has confirmed Machiavelli's insight of 600 years ago: Fear of loss is a more powerful factor in human behavior than the drive for gain. This is especially true for elites, a risk-averse bunch, who often feel that they have a lot to lose by any change in direction.

Experienced diplomats know that countries, even though they have agreed to join or at least not oppose a coalition, play a variety of roles with varying degrees of commitment to the coalition's goal. Some are enthusiastic *partisans*. Some are cautious *joiners*. Some are *cruisers*, just along for the ride, ready to jump off the coalition when it encounters difficulties. Some are *neutrals* who don't oppose the coalition but at the same time don't work to achieve its goals. And of course, some are *spoilers*, who while not expressing overt opposition to the visionary coalition, nonetheless won't miss an opportunity to weaken or destroy it.[5]

In organizations, persons who have in one way or other indicated their support for the direction—the vision—that the leader has negotiated with them also play the same assortment of roles as do countries in coalitions. Agreement to a vision does not necessarily mean strong commitment to it. As a result, a leader, often using one-on-one encounters, must make a hard-headed assessment of the degree of genuine commitment that each follower may have to pursuing the new direction seemingly agreed upon.

Beware of becoming so intoxicated by your own vision for the organization and the sense of your own charisma and authority that you fail to see clearly the reservations and hesitations that members of your organization may have about pursuing that vision enthusiastically. When an organization member says, "Yes, but . . ." to the vision, too often enthusiastic leaders seize on the "yes" but miss the "but."

Sometimes members of your organization will state their reservations and hesitations openly; sometimes they may not. In the latter case, you need to look for tell-tale signs indicating less than genuine commitment. For example, is a member who normally participates actively in meetings curiously silent about new directions and visions for the organization? Has another member declined to join task forces or committees working on the new vision? Or, if he has accepted membership, has he frequently missed its meetings? Does the normally enthusiastic, sprightly, free-wheeling conversationalist become uncharacteristically reserved when the subject of the organization's new vision and direction arises?

> Beware of becoming so intoxicated by your own vision that you fail to see clearly the reservations that members of your organization may have about pursuing that vision enthusiastically.

Even though an organization may have adopted a new direction by a unanimous vote, an experienced leader of leaders learns to recognize and interpret these signs to mean that some one-on-one leadership with these persons will be required in order to strengthen their commitment to the strategic decision that the organization has taken.

The process of one-on-one commitment strengthening follows most of the principles that we previously discussed in Chapter 3 on the art of strategic conversation. So a first step in commitment strengthening is to understand why the persons you are hoping to lead in a new direction have hesitations or reservations. That understanding will help you develop an approach to easing those concerns, thereby hopefully strengthening commitment to the new direction.

Overseeing Direction

An organization not only expects its leaders to help them determine and then commit to a direction, but also to ensure that the organization actually moves in the direction it has adopted. The process of direction oversight is crucial to an organization's success. Understand that no strategic plan can predict the future with absolute accuracy. While pressing forward with determination to move the organization in a desired direction, you must also be ready to recognize and deal with the unexpected, perhaps to slow down movement toward, halt progress completely, or veer away from the direction that the organization had previously adopted.

Citigroup, under the leadership and vision of Sanford Weill, its chairman and CEO, had aggressively moved in the 1990s to make itself the leading financial services institution in the world. With the beginning of the twenty-first century, it experienced a series of financial scandals that led regulators in the United States and abroad to impose severe penalties on the organization, a situation that threatened to damage the Citigroup brand in the market place. As a result, the Citigroup board named Charles O. Prince as CEO, and his task as leader was not to create a new vision for the organization but to assure compliance with the law and business ethics, goals that Citigroup had presumably always declared were part of its mission and direction.[6]

The leadership task of determining, securing commitment to, and overseeing progress toward a direction for an organization is thus a basic yet complex task of leadership. It is particularly complex when you are leading other leaders, as was the case when Goldman Sachs, the great Wall Street investment bank, made a strategic decision to adopt a new direction in 1998.

Negotiating a Vision for Goldman Sachs

Goldman Sachs is probably the most successful investment bank in the world. Founded in New York City in 1869 by Marcus Goldman, a

German immigrant who set up shop as a broker of commercial IOUs in lower Manhattan, the firm would grow to become an international financial powerhouse. By the end of the twentieth century, the firm had masterminded some the major deals of the century, including the Ford Motor Company's initial public offering in 1956, the privatization of British Petroleum in 1987, General Electric's acquisition of RCA in 1986, the $13 billion privatization of Deutche Telecom (the largest IPO ever undertaken) in 1996, and the $38 billion merger of Daimler Benz and Chrysler Corporation in 1998, the largest industrial merger. The firm's success has been attributed to three consistent factors over the years: its leadership, its people, and its culture.[7] To a significant extent, its singular culture and its ability to attract excellent people were dependent on the special structure that it maintained throughout the twentieth century—a private partnership.

In 1986, 80 percent of the capital of this $38 billion business was owned by its 104 active partners, with the remaining 20 percent held by retired partners. The partnership structure gave the firm several distinct advantages over the years. First, the fact that it was private meant that it did not have to respond to the vicissitudes of the stock market but instead could undertake long-term, profitable strategies that the shareholders of public traded firms would not have tolerated. As one of its partners was fond of saying, "Greedy, but long-term greedy."

Second, as a private firm, it was not subject to the reporting requirements of publicly held corporations. This fostered a culture of confidentiality that not only served the partners, but their clients as well. Goldman Sachs developed a strong client-oriented culture that resulted in enduring and extremely lucrative business relationships.

Third, since the net worth of the partners was to a large extent based on their ownership interest in the firm, and since its growth depended on firm profitability, the partnership structure fostered a culture of teamwork among the partners, a factor that was an important reason for the firm's financial success. It also engendered a high degree of trust and commitment among the partners to the all-consuming task of the partnership business.

Fourth, the prospect of becoming a partner at Goldman Sachs was a key factor in the firm's ability to hire, retain, and motivate some of the best and brightest financial talent in the world. Not only would a partnership result in considerable wealth to a recipient, but a Goldman Sachs partnership came to have a special cachet on Wall Street—a cachet that meant its recipient was among the elite of the financial world. As a result, Goldman Sachs partners included some of the smartest, most talented, richest, and most powerful people on Wall Street.

But if the partnership structure had served the firm well for nearly a hundred-and-thirty years, by the 1980s it also began to reveal some disadvantages. First, it rendered the firm's capital base unstable. Whenever partners withdrew or retired from the firm, they took their share of the capital with them. Second, a partnership meant that the growth of the firm's capital depended largely on retained earnings. The partnership structure prevented it from raising large amounts of capital from the stock market in order to take advantage of new business opportunities that were emerging as a result of globalization. Third, and perhaps most constraining of all, being a partnership meant that Goldman Sachs, unlike all of its competitors, which had one by one become publicly held corporations, could not make acquisitions through the issuance of stock and thus could not grow rapidly.

Moreover, because of the partnership structure, the partners, unlike shareholders, were personally liable for all of the firm's obligations, a factor that came to be of increasing concern as mammoth lawsuits struck the financial industry with growing frequency. And finally, an initial public offering would result in considerable personal enrichment for the Goldman Sachs partners, particularly the more senior partners, whose capital accounts had grown as a result of the firm's accumulated profits.

Goldman Searches for a New Direction

Because of these factors, the leadership of Goldman Sachs, beginning in the 1960s, considered from time to time the possibility of converting the firm to a corporation and making an initial public offering of its shares. Finally, in 1986, the firm's nine-person management committee formally recommended to the ninety-five other partners that Goldman Sachs make this fundamental strategic change. The management committee, which included Robert Rubin, soon to be co-vice chairman of Goldman Sachs and later, U.S. Secretary of the Treasury during the Clinton administration, was in effect presenting a new vision for the firm, setting a new direction to enable the firm to attain the goal of becoming the preeminent investment bank in a rapidly globalizing world.

Over a weekend in December 1986, all of the partners, slightly more than 100 in number, met to consider this vital proposed change in direction. Prior to the meeting, Rubin and his colleagues on the management committee had sought to lobby key senior partners in support of the proposal to go public. In competing organizations that had already taken a similar decision, the leadership had faced the members with a *fait accompli* and had merely asked them to give formal approval. That approach was rejected at Goldman Sachs. For one thing, it would have violated the ingrained culture of teamwork and collegiality that had been so assiduously developed over the years. For another, it might have prompted key partners to leave the firm, depriving it of vital capital and talents, rendering Goldman even less able to compete in the new, dawning financial world.

For two days, the partners debated the proposal, often with high emotion. Opposition to the idea of an initial public offering was strong, perhaps stronger than the management committee had anticipated. At the end of two days, without a formal vote being taken, the committee and the other partners saw clearly that there was no consensus for going public. The meeting was ended with no decision, which meant that Goldman Sachs would remain a partnership.

Various reasons have been advanced for the failure of the firm's leadership to arrive at an agreement on a new direction in 1986. First, the formal proposal was not well prepared. The partnership included some of the most financially astute persons in the world and they quickly applied their talents to challenging much of the financial analysis that underlay the proposal. Second, a shift from the traditional culture of Goldman Sachs—characterized by teamwork, privacy, and solidarity, a culture that they all valued highly—to the unknowns of a publicly traded corporation was just not one that the partners were psychologically prepared to make, despite the fact that an IPO would make many partners much richer than they already were.

While some partners believed that a publicly traded structure would have net advantages and some believed it to be a net loss, all partners regretted the change of culture that a public offering would entail. In addition, the firm had taken in an unusually large group of 37 new partners in 1986. Having had no time to accumulate equity in the first year, they stood to gain little from an IPO, and they therefore uniformly opposed it. An IPO was simply not in their interest. And finally, although the management committee had put forward the proposal for an IPO to the group, it did not aggressively push to secure its adoption with the other partners. Rather, the committee advanced the idea, listened to what the partners had to say, and in the face of strong opposition, ultimately withdrew.

On the one hand, the 1986 meeting could be seen as a rejection of the proposed new direction by the firm's leadership. On the other hand, all the partners left the meeting knowing that the issue was far from dead, and that the conversation about the firm's future had really just begun. At the same time, in retrospect, the partners seemed to have adopted the vision of Rubin and the other management committee members that Goldman Sachs's basic goal was to become a "world-class financial organization."

Under New Leadership, the Search for a New Direction Continues

Ten years later, with the firm now under the leadership of Jon Corzine, who would within a short time be elected to the U.S. Senate from New Jersey, the Goldman Sachs partners once again considered a proposal to become a publicly traded corporation and abandon its traditional partnership structure. In the interim, as discussion continued among the partners, the firm had instituted a variety of internal changes and raised capital from outside through private placements. The firm also encountered various problems, one of which was the fact that increasing numbers of partners were withdrawing from the firm and taking their capital with them. To counter this threat, Corzine and the firm leadership believed that an IPO would stabilize the firm's capital and allow it to retain its talent, Goldman Sachs' primary asset. Therefore, to avoid repeating one of the mistakes of the 1986 meeting, prior to the 1996 partners meeting, a special committee was appointed to prepare, in great detail, a complete proposal for an initial public offering.

The world of finance had changed significantly during the preceding decade. Goldman Sachs had grown in size and scope, but its members realized that it still had to grow even more through the process of acquisitions if it was to attain its goal of becoming a world-class financial firm. Potential objections to an IPO were anticipated and arguments made to counter them. In addition, Corzine and the leadership engaged in extensive "pre-selling" with other partners before the meeting took place. Once again, an all-weekend meeting took place among the partners to consider the future of the firm through extensive discussions. By Sunday, it had become clear to Corzine and the executive committee that the partners did not want to sell the firm, so they withdrew the IPO proposal from consideration. Their reasons were the same as those advanced in 1986, but due to the depressed state of the stock market, the partners probably also concluded that the premium to be gained by an IPO was not worth the cost of losing their valued firm culture.

The 1996 meeting was not, however, a total defeat. First, it served to further educate the partners about all the implications of an IPO. As a result, discussions about the firm's future directions would continue after the meeting. Second, and perhaps more important, the partners authorized Corzine and the executive committee to take a variety of measures to alter the firm's structure, all of which would facilitate an eventual IPO. Thus, the firm was converted from a partnership to a limited liability company and it ceased to use the term "partner" to designate its members. Henceforth, all partners (as well as hundreds of the firm's other highest executives) would be designated managing directors, who would have all the rights and privileges of partners, except that they owned no equity in the firm. Moreover, partnership rules on withdrawal of capital were changed to give increased stability to the firm's capital base. It was also understood that in the future the firm would periodically revisit the question of whether to go public.

In 1998—just two years later—the leadership decided it was time to revisit the issue of going public. Two powerful intervening forces prompted this decision. First, the stock market had experienced spectacular growth, causing the firm to be worth much more than in 1996 and potentially enabling individual partners to reap significant financial rewards from an IPO. Second, and even more important for the future of Goldman Sachs, many of the firm's principal competitors had rapidly grown into global giants through mergers and acquisitions, primarily by issuing stock. Goldman Sachs, because of its structure, had been unable to grow in the same manner. The size, breadth, and global reach of these new financial institutions, it was feared, would put Goldman Sachs at a competitive disadvantage that would only grow over time.

In response, the management committee established a subcommittee to review the firm's strategy in this new and rapidly changing business environment. The subcommittee's goal was not to recommend whether to go public, but rather to propose a business strategy that the firm should adopt. "Structure follows strategy" was the group's watchword, and this was made clear to all of the Goldman partners. The subcommittee was to look forward ten years and decide what kind of a firm Goldman Sachs was to become at the end of that time. As it undertook this study, it realized that the firm's most important strategic question was how fast to grow. Ultimately, the committee recommended a program of aggressive growth, doubling the number of people engaged in the client-service portion of the business in just five years.

Having set out that strategic goal, it then outlined the various ways in which the firm might attain this goal, one of which was by going public. Their recommendations were then presented to all the partners, and the firm scheduled yet another partnership meeting to consider them. During the intervening period, Corzine, now joined as co-chairman by Hank Paulson, engaged in one-on-one conversations with nearly all of the firm's 190 partners.

In June 1998, for the third time in twelve years, all the partners of Goldman Sachs convened in a weekend retreat to consider the strategic proposal and the means to implement it. The session began with a general presentation by Paulson of the proposal. But rather than making a hard sell in favor of an IPO, Paulson very carefully discussed the pros and cons of the proposal, raising all the hard questions that the partners had to satisfy themselves about. His goal was not to sell an idea but to make his fellow partners think hard about what was in the best interests of the firm. After Paulson's presentation, the partners broke up into small working groups known as "echo tutorials," whose purpose was to give them a deeper understanding of the proposed strategic direction's implications. Informal conversation about the future continued among the partners over dinner in the evening.

The next day Corzine made a presentation about the question of the fairness of the proposal to go public and also read a letter from two distinguished former partners who opposed a change in structure. Thereafter, the floor was turned over to the partners for their views. More than 100 partners spoke, expressing both approval and opposition to the idea of selling the firm to the public. Finally, on Saturday afternoon, the partners were given a ballot, asking which ownership structure they preferred and why. The meeting then adjourned, and the executive committee convened to consider the views expressed by their colleagues. The Goldman leadership had decided in advance that any new strategy had such momentous consequences for the firm that a mere majority of partners would not be enough to make the change. Instead, a supermajority would be needed.

Goldman Finally Finds a New Direction

The following Monday, the executive committee announced that it had been decided to sell the firm's shares to the public. After thirteen years, numerous meetings, and virtually endless discussions, Goldman Sachs, an organization consisting of some of the smartest, most talented, richest, and most powerful people in the financial world, finally decided to adopt a significant new strategic direction for their venerable firm.[8] The public offering itself did not take place immediately. Right after the decision was made, the stock market experienced downward pressure. The firm leadership, exercising discretion and oversight, deferred the IPO until May 1999.

Goldman's decision to go public did not just happen. The firm was led to make that decision through the efforts of its leaders. On the one hand, leaders like Robert Rubin and Jon Corzine knew that the firm needed to seek a new strategic direction because of significant changes taking place in the world. On the other hand, they also realized that they themselves could not force that decision on the partners. Rather over time, they had to negotiate agreement on a new vision for the firm, and build a coalition among the partners to support it. In short, as leaders leading other leaders, they had to play the role of visionary diplomats, rather than visionary prophets, if their organization was to make a vital change of direction.

You may ask: Did it have to take so long? Could other leaders have achieved the same result in less time? Would the prototypical, dynamic corporate CEO—a Jack Welch, a Louis Gerstner, or a Sandy Weill—have done a more effective job of leading Goldman Sachs to a new strategic vision than a Rubin or a Corzine? The answer to that question is: Almost certainly not. The Goldman Sachs partners, by virtue of the fact that they owned the firm, had the power to say "no" to any proposal, to remove from leadership anyone who they felt threatened their interests, and to replace that person with someone who better served them.

In the Goldman Sachs situation, it was not vision and charisma that would lead leaders, but an understanding of the partners' interests and an ability to convince them that a needed new direction advanced those interests. The strategic change at Goldman Sachs was an example of interest-based leadership of the highest order.

Basic Principles for Negotiating a Direction

Although the Goldman Sachs case is special, in many ways it does illustrate some basic principles about the way to lead leaders to find and adopt a new direction. Here are a few principles that should guide you.

1. *Determine a direction for elite followers by structuring and conducting a strategic conversation.* For Goldman Sachs, determining a new direction for the firm was the product of a conversation that took thirteen years. For most organizations composed of leaders, finding a strategic direction is also the product of a conversation. The basic task of the leadership is to structure and conduct that conversation, rather than to try to impose a new vision from the top. While few organizations will require thirteen years to find their way as Goldman did, it is important to realize that conducting a strategic conversation among leaders about organizational direction can be time consuming and often frustrating.

2. *Develop a fair process for conducting the conversation about direction.* If you as the leader have a clear vision of the organization's future and a distinct sense of the best direction to follow, resist the temptation to try to impose it on your organization. As Machiavelli noted 600 years ago, the dangers for a leader in trying to impose a new order is that you will make enemies of those who benefited from the old order and gain only lukewarm support from those who stand to benefit from

the new. In the end your enemies may prevent you from imposing your new order, and even if you overcome them they will remain opponents as you go about the process of implementing it. This does not mean, of course, that you abandon any hope of moving the organization in a more productive direction. Rather, it means that you need to find and develop a process that will enable the organization's members to participate in determining new directions. In the Goldman Sachs case, the firm worked out a definite process of meetings and consultations to help the partners arrive at a new strategic direction.

Leaders often become impatient with process. They want to get things done, to get the organization moving in the right direction as quickly as possible. Worrying about process, they think, merely delays the important tasks of leadership. Moreover, many leaders feel that becoming embroiled in process makes them look weak and indecisive and gives their opponents within the organization an opportunity to undermine them. But developing the right process for determining organizational direction is essential for several reasons.

First, as research has shown, people are more likely to accept and act on a decision if they believe it resulted from a fair process, even if they do not fully agree with that decision, than if that decision was imposed from above or resulted from an unfair process. Second, effective process will allow you to tap fully the resources of your organization. Smart, talented, rich, and powerful people usually have valuable ideas, experience, and knowledge that you can profitably use in determining the direction for your organization. Admit it: there are people in your organization who know a lot more than you do. Third, involving the members of your organization meaningfully in the process of direction setting is a concrete signal that you respect them and their ideas and is thus an important element in gaining their trust, an essential asset if you are to lead the organization effectively.

> You need to find and develop a process that will enable the organization's members to participate in determining new directions.

And fourth, good process gives legitimacy to decisions on new directions.

No matter how much charisma you have, some members of an organization may remain opposed to the new direction, or at most offer very lukewarm support. However, they are less likely to be able to thwart or sabotage those new directions when decisions on directions have emerged from a fair process than if you had had handed them down by fiat like a Machiavellian Prince. And finally, the existence of a fair process for direction setting may serve to place a check on the charismatic leader whose vision for the organization—for example rapid acquisition of unrelated businesses—is essentially self-serving as a means to increase an empire over which that leader hopes to rule.[9]

3. *Establish a fair process that includes the opportunity for followers' genuine participation and decisions based on acceptable principles and standards.* The process by which Goldman Sachs arrived at a decision to adopt a new strategic direction was based first of all on the full participation of all the partners in the deliberations. All partners had the right to speak, and all were sincerely encouraged to do so. They exercised that right throughout the thirteen years that the decision was under consideration.

The goal of the conversation is not merely to determine a direction but to cause the members of the organization to adopt, believe in, and work enthusiastically toward the direction that is decided. Ownership of the decision by members of the group is a key to success. Ownership is much more likely to result if the members played a part in making the decision on direction than if the organization's leaders arrived at *their* desired result by manipulating, short-circuiting, or dominating the process.

4. *Once you have established a process, use it genuinely to help determine a direction for your organization.* Sometimes leaders put in place a process of consultation that is merely a charade, a means to justify what they wanted to do in the first place. Smart, talented, rich, and power-

ful people will quickly come to know when they are engaged in meaningless activity. Once they do realize that they are involved in a purely formal process that has little or no significance, they will also participate in a purely formal way, if at all.

During the Soviet era, Russian workers jokingly explained their less than diligent work habits by saying: "They pretend to pay us, so we pretend to work." Similarly, followers asked to participate in a process that will have no influence on the organization's direction are likely to say, referring to their leaders, "They pretend to have an interest in our ideas, so we pretend to tell them."

5. *Your primary function as a leader is to ask the right questions.* Traditionally, leaders have seen their function as pointing the way, as indicating, if not formally *ordering*, a definite path for the organization to follow. In leading leaders, however, the most effective instrument is not an order but the right question. The leadership of Goldman Sachs, after two failed attempts to convince the partners to go public, reframed the question that they were to answer from "Should the firm go public?" to "What should be the firm's strategy in the radically changed financial environment at the end of the twentieth century?" This was a question that affected the vital interests of the firm and all its partners. It was a question that was designed to elicit the strong and positive participation of all. Once the firm had answered the basic questions by deciding to be a world-class financial firm, it then had to face the question of finding the resources to compete with much larger competitors. This question, in turn, led the partners to decide on going public.

6. *Discern patterns of deference.* Within a group of leaders, some are more influential than others. Among the Goldman Sachs partners, some had more influence on their colleagues than others. The effort of determining and adopting a direction for a group of leaders is similar to building a coalition

> In leading leaders, the most effective instrument is not an order but the right question.

in a diplomatic conference or a legislature. Some leaders, like some countries or some legislators, may be more influential in the process than others. Moreover, even if individual partners have little influence, they may enhance their clout by forming blocks or coalitions, as the 37 new Goldman partners did to considerable effect in the 1986 meeting. It is therefore important for a leader of leaders conducting the conversation on direction, as two scholars have said, "to discern patterns of deference" among the members of the group to be led and then to mobilize those patterns to arrive at an agreement on strategic directions.[10]

While all leaders, such as the partners at Goldman Sachs or ambassadors at a conference, would reject the notion that they are subject to the authority of another leader, ambassador, or partner, they are nonetheless willing in many cases to "defer"—that is to be influenced by—the views and opinions of certain of their colleagues. The source of that deference among theoretically autonomous equals may be derived from many factors—a personal relationship, seniority, favors done in the past, or benefits expected in the future. The effective leader of leaders not only seeks to discern those patterns of deference but to understand their basis and then to use them to achieve organizational goals.

Conclusion: Rules for Achieving the Task of Direction

To help you to lead leaders to find and adopt a new direction, here is a summary of the rules that should guide you:

1. To determine a direction for elite followers, structure and conduct a strategic conversation on that subject, rather than impose a new vision from the top.

2. Develop a fair process for conducting the conversation about direction.

3. Make sure the process allows for the genuine participation of followers, and for decisions based on acceptable principles and standards.

4. Once you have established a process, use it genuinely to help determine a direction for your organization.

5. Remember that one of your primary functions as a leader providing direction is to ask the right questions.

6. Learn to discern "patterns of deference" among the members of the group you lead and then mobilize those patterns to arrive at an agreement on strategic direction.

Notes

1. Henry Miller, *The Wisdom of the Heart* (1941).

2. See, for example, Balajis Chakravarthy and Peter Lorane, *Managing the Strategy Process: A Framework for a Multibusiness Firm* (Englewood Cliffs, N.J.: Prentice Hall, 1991), p. 15.

3. See Jeswald W. Salacuse, "Corporate Governance, Culture, and Convergence: Corporations American Style or with a European Touch?" *Law and Business Review of the Americas* 9, 33 (2003).

4. *The Prince*, translated by N. H. Thomson (New York: Dover Publications, 1992), p. 13.

5. For a conceptual discussion of coalition building and the various roles parties may play in a coalition, see Christophe DuPont, "Negotiation as Coalition Building," *International Negotiation* 1 (1996), pp. 47-64.

6. Timothy O'Brien and Landon Thomas, Jr., "It's Cleanup Time at Citi," *New York Times*, November 7, 2004, Section 3, p. 1.

7. Lisa Endlich, *Goldman Sachs: The Culture of Success* (New York: Simon and Schuster, 2000), p. vii.

8. For an excellent history of Goldman Sachs and its decision to go public, see Lisa Endlich, *Goldman Sachs: The Culture of Success* (2000).

9. See Yassin Sanher, "Character Not Charisma Is the Critical Mea-

sure of Leadership Excellence," *Journal of Leadership and Organizational Studies* 9, 47 (2003).

10. Lance N. Antrim and James K. Sebenius, "Formal Individual Mediation and the Negotiators' Dilemma: Tommy Koh at the Law of the Sea Conference," in Bercovitch and Rubin, eds., *Mediation in International Relations: Multiple Approaches to Conflict Management* (New York: St Martin's Press, 1992), p. 124.

Task No. 2: Integration

Making Stars a Team

> The multitude that does not become a unity is confusion;
> the unity that does not depend on the multitude is tyranny.
>
> —Blaise Pascal

A FEW DAYS into my tenure as dean of the Southern Methodist University Law School, a senior member of the faculty with whom I had been friendly, told me that he considered the dean's role to be "custodial in nature." My job, as far as he was concerned, was to keep the buildings operating and the staff responsive, and let the faculty get on with the essential work of teaching students and doing research. Hospital administrators, law firm managing partners, managing directors of financial services firms, and university presidents should not be overly disappointed if the people in their own organizations have similar views about the custodial nature of their leadership. Indeed, anyone whose job is to lead leaders understands that a fundamental task is to enable those persons to apply their special abilities to the fullest. Sometimes the best way you can do that is to keep the building warm and lighted.

The Follower's Dilemma

Smart, talented, rich, and powerful people usually have a strong sense of their own independence. Board members, doctors, lawyers, investment bankers, and university professors view their success as depending essentially on their own skills and their own achievements. Money managers, architects, senators, judges, and wealthy entrepreneurs, too, because of their education, talents, money, and political connections, have a strong sense of individualism and self-worth that they do not readily subordinate to the will of other persons, including someone whose title means that they are supposed to lead them.

For these persons, regardless of their professional area of expertise, belonging to an organization is often a convenience that enables them to achieve their personal goals, and the designated leader of that organization works best when he or she facilitates the attainment of those goals. If for some reason, the current organization to which they belong doesn't meet their needs, there are always other organizations they can join. They are stars. Like star professional athletes in their prime, they can always move on to another team. After all, didn't Roger Clemens excel as a pitcher with the Boston Red Sox, the Toronto Blue Jays, the New York Yankees, *and* the Houston Astros?

The same professor, who had described my job as "custodial," sometime later in talking about a particularly difficult issue that had divided the faculty would stress to me quite forcefully that as dean I needed to "bring us together, to unify us." He now clearly felt that in addition to keeping the buildings warm and lighted, I also had the task of integrating the faculty as an effective working organization. My job was to unite the group, to create a community of diverse, talented, and very smart individuals who at the same time held fiercely to their sense of independence. In short my job, like that of an NBA coach or a major league baseball manager, was somehow to make stars a team.

In conceptual terms, making stars a team is a task of integration. Integration is a process of combining various parts or elements into a more harmonious, effective, and productive unit, and by this process, somehow make the whole greater than the sum of its parts. An integrated team, whether in baseball or investment banking, usually performs its tasks, whether winning games or launching IPOs, more efficiently and effectively than one that is beset by conflict and tur-moil. An integrated team may seize opportunities to create value that would elude a collection of individual stars. An integrated law firm, by mobilizing the diverse talents and specialties of its members, can serve a variety of client needs and thereby generate more income for the firm than if individual star lawyers work with clients only in their area of specialization and show no concern for problems outside of that specialization. And an integrated think tank or research institute is more likely to undertake innovative studies across disciplinary boundaries than is a group of star scholars laboring separately in their own offices and laboratories with little contact with one another. Lack of integration, on the other hand, can lead to friction within the orga-nization that actually hinders the ability of that organization to serve individual stars in the best way possible.

Psychologists have found that all people have two basic social needs: a need for autonomy and a need to belong.[1] The degree to which specific individuals will seek these two goals and the priority they attach to each depends on a variety of factors, including personal-ity, culture, and context. Some persons with what psychologists call an "independent self-construal," tend to define themselves in terms of the attributes, preferences, and traits that make them unique and autonomous from their social world, while other persons having an interdependent self-view tend to define themselves in terms of their social relationships and group memberships.[2]

Similarly, members of an organization will generally recognize that some degree of integration is important for their organizations, and they almost always look to leaders to undertake this vital task. They will often differ however on the desired *degree* of organizational integration necessary and the price they are willing to pay for it in terms of reduced personal autonomy. As a result, the dilemma that all followers face in an organization is: How much should I cooperate with the leadership to allow integration to happen and how much should I assert my own individual interests so that I can pursue my own professional goals? That in effect is the follower's dilemma, and every leader needs to recognize that all of the organization's members address this question either consciously or subconsciously every day.

The follower's dilemma creates a constant tension between the drive to assert individual interests and the drive to assert organizational interests. It is the dilemma of choosing between individual independence and organizational integration, of responding to the universal human needs of autonomy and belonging. The principal task of the leader in high-talent organizations is to convince all members of the organization that their primary interests lie in successful organizational integration and that they should therefore cooperate with, support, help and, indeed, initiate efforts to integrate the organization's members into a dynamic team.

Many highly talented individuals may have a tendency towards "independent self-construal." So leaders of high-talent organizations may find that they are called upon to lead a higher percentage of persons for whom autonomy is a primary goal than they would find in other kinds of organizations. As a result, you need to shape your integration strategies accordingly.

Integration happens as members come to feel that they are part of a community, that they share certain things, and that as a group they hold certain values, ideas, and especially interests in common. More important, integration is driven by a growing realization among an organization's members that an integrated organization meets their interests better than one that is not integrated. Integration evolves as working relations are established among the organization's members. A relationship is a feeling that one person has of being connected or linked in some way to another person. In an integrated organization, those links and connections are multiple and strong. In organizations that lack integration, those relationships either do not exist or are dysfunctional.

> The follower's dilemma creates a constant tension between the drive to assert individual interests and the drive to assert organizational interests.

In that regard, an integrated organization is like a complicated electronic circuit that links together the various electronic components that allow a computer to function properly. One of the tasks of a leader is to help to create that sense of community, to help its members identify and articulate what they have in common, to remind them of what they share together. A leader, like a computer engineer, works to establish, maintain, and strengthen the circuitry—the relationships—that allow the organization to function as an integrated mechanism, rather than to be a jumble of unconnected components sitting in a box on a workbench.

At the same time, leaders of high-talent organizations must recognize that the needed *degree* of integration may vary, depending on the nature of the firm, the particular goal it seeks to achieve, the nature of the external environment at a given time in history, and the perceived interests of the organization's members. Forcing integration for its own sake without regard to the perceived interests and needed independence of the organization's members to do their jobs appropriately may in the end reduce the effectiveness of the organization. The balance between individual independence and organizational integration, which is at the heart of the follower's dilemma, is one that a leader of a high-talent organization has to manage carefully and constantly.

Barriers to Integration

Like computer engineers diagnosing the causes for the failure of an electronic circuit, leaders undertaking the task of integration need to identify at the outset the barriers to integration that exist in their organizations and then develop strategies and tactics for dealing with them. Here are some of the principal barriers to integration that leaders encounter in high-talent organizations:

1. No Perceived Common Interests

Interests drive actions. If the stars you are supposed to lead feel they have few common interests, they are not likely to work in an integrated fashion. The prevailing attitude among them will be: "You do your thing and I'll do mine." Star doctors, lawyers, asset managers, or management consultants who are compensated exclusively and richly on the basis of revenues generated from their own patients, clients, or accounts, will often feel that firm-wide activities like staff recruitment and strategic planning have little interest for them and therefore will seek to spend as little time as possible on those activities.

2. Lack of a Felt Shared History

A sense of a common history is a powerful force for the integration of groups, whether they are professional organizations or nations. All countries encourage or require the teaching of history in schools in order to create a sense of unity and of integration among its citizens. One of the first challenges to integrating an organization is often the fact that its members do not feel that they have any shared history. Or they may believe that if there is a history of working together, it is really not important with respect to what each individual in the organization is doing today.

3. Too Much Bad History

The members of an organization may indeed have a shared history, but they may view that history negatively. As a result, that history may serve to divide rather than to unite, to separate rather than to integrate the members of the organization. A nation that has endured a civil war will often find that the memory of the pains endured and the humiliation experienced in the conflict will remain in the memory of its people for generations and serve as a continuing cause of divisiveness. Similarly, the remembrance by an organization's members of past internal quarrels, struggles for power, heated arguments over policy, and contested personnel decisions can become part of the organization's folklore and serve as a continuing source of hostility and distrust among persons who otherwise might have considered themselves colleagues. That distrust and hostility effectively serves to inhibit integration. For example, the contested decision by the Columbia University administration to ask the New York City Police to intervene in the student sit-ins and protests of 1968 led to internal divisions that persisted long after the Vietnam War had ended.

4. Poor Internal Communication

If integration requires connection among components, that connection in organizations is the ongoing process of communication. Poor or nonexistent communication within organizations means that individual members do not know what other members are doing, and so the necessary connection for integration among them is missing.

Perhaps even more pernicious than no communication is unequal communication, a situation where some organization members receive vital firm-wide information and others don't. Knowledge is indeed power. A situation of unequal distribution of information will mean that some members who are privy to vital information will gain influence in the organization, and that those without access will feel disempowered, a result that will only heighten the lack of integration.

5. Cultural Differences

An important barrier that prevents stars from functioning as a team is a difference in culture among its members. What do we mean by culture? *Culture* consists of the behavior patterns, attitudes, norms, and values of a given community. Nations have cultures and so do organizations. At it most simple level, culture is "the way we do things around here."

Individuals in high talent organizations develop a culture from one or more of three distinct sources: from their national background, from their previous organizational experience, and from their professional training. Hans Brandt, the German computer engineer we met earlier who had arrived on the scene as a result of an acquisition, clearly had a different culture from the other members of his new company. But differences in culture within organizations are not the product of national differences alone. They are more often the product of different organizational and professional cultures.

Some organizations, like Goldman Sachs, with a deep sense of history and tradition, have over time developed a culture that its members value and that gives the organization strong cohesion. On the other hand, new organizations or organizations that have been formed by the merger or acquisition of existing firms often find that their members have different cultures—different behavior patterns, attitudes, norms, and values about work, organization, and life that effectively prevent them from acting in an integrated way.

Professionally trained persons—whether they are doctors, lawyers, management consultants, or clergy—have not only gained specialized knowledge and skills from their education. They have also gained a culture—a set of distinct behavior patterns, attitudes, and values about their work, the organizations in which they do their work, and indeed about life itself. In organizations composed of persons with different professional training and background, for example lawyers and engineers or scientists and management consultants, differences in culture may arise that cause internal conflict or inhibit effective action.

Culture can influence the way work is done, indeed the very way work is perceived by the members of an organization: how meetings are conducted, how people communicate with one another, how work is rewarded, and how teams function. In an organization like Goldman Sachs, whose culture has evolved over more than a hundred years and is carefully taught to its new members, this common culture gives a strong impetus for organizational integration. An organization without a common ac-

An organization without a common accepted culture may experience constant conflict, miscommunications, disappointed expectations, and dysfunction.

cepted culture may experience constant conflict, miscommunications, disappointed expectations, and therefore dysfunction in the form of poor performance and the failure to take full advantage of opportunities in the market.

6. Spoilers

Different individuals within high-talent organizations may view the prospect of integration differently. Some may see it as a way of enhancing the organization and therefore promoting their own interests. Others may view it as a threat to their interests and therefore seek to prevent it. For example, organization members who are profiting from the status quo handsomely would not want to see greater integration among firm members if that meant that the leadership would gain support to make policy changes not in their interests. These persons are "spoilers." A spoiler's basic tactic is to prevent change by blocking agreement—that is, integration—by the other members of the organization. Sometimes a leader can easily identify spoilers by their actions; sometimes spoilers effectively hide their intentions and actions from the leadership and from the other members.

7. Divide-and-Conquer Leadership

In many organizations, the barrier to integration is the leadership itself, either past or present. An age-old leadership strategy is "divide-and-conquer," a method used not only by colonial rulers but by many modern-day managers. Divide-and-conquer leaders view unity among a group's members, whether they are Nigerian tribes or portfolio managers, as a threat to their own power. Therefore, in order to gain or preserve their influence, some leaders will deliberately seek to foster competition among their subordinates and actively prevent actions that would otherwise facilitate integration among the organization's members.

So instead of encouraging full and open communication within

the organization, a divide-and-conquer leader will provide information selectively to certain groups and not to others. Instead of encouraging cohesion among the membership of a high-talent organization,
a divide-and conquer leader will favor some groups over others—for
example, the traders as opposed to the dealmakers in an investment
bank—and thereby assure the loyalty of the favored group in future
contested decisions and actions. As a leader in a high-talent organization, you may not be a practitioner of divide-and-conquer leadership,
but if your predecessor practiced this art, one of your challenges may
be to find ways to undo its consequences within the organization.

Removing the Barriers to Integration

Integration of high-talent organizations, the process of making stars a
team, requires leaders to find ways to remove these integration barriers. You cannot sweep them away by eloquent speeches at company
meetings or stern memorandums from the executive suite. To a significant extent, their removal will require you as a leader to engage in
one-on-one strategic conversations with the persons you lead. Persons
who resist integration by insisting on their autonomy at the expense
of the group, are exercising their personal power to defend their interests. Psychologists have found that the existence of a relationship between a person with more power and another person with less power
tends to moderate the use of that power.[3] What you as a leader are
seeking to do through one-one-one interactions is to create relationships among the persons you lead and thus moderate their exercise of
personal power in favor of organizational interests.

If lack of organizational integration is akin to unconnected electronic components sitting on a workbench, how should a leader of
leaders go about connecting them to create integrated circuits within
the organization? Here are a few techniques that may help.

1. Make Common Interests Apparent Through Meaningful Activity

Elite followers, such as doctors, architects, and management consultants, quite naturally focus first and foremost on the work they were

trained to do, whether it is heart transplants, high-rise designs, or corporate reorganizations. They view their basic interests, both personal and professional, as doing the work for which they were trained. In most cases, their education did not equip them specifically to work in organizations, and they probably have given little serious thought to the organizational needs of their professions and their employers. They may see little connection between what they do and what others in the organization do or indeed what the organization as a whole does.

Recognizing that stars on a team and professionals in high-talent organizations respond to their perceived interests, one tactic of leaders seeking greater integration is to make their colleagues in the organization appreciate that their interests will be advanced if the organization becomes more integrated. One way to achieve this goal is to involve them in activities that will enable them to perceive this potential for interest advancement. For example, their participation in committees related to the governance of the organization may foster integration, even though some leaders may view this activity as interfering with leadership prerogatives. Governance committees make clear to the members of the organization that they have a definite stake in an integrated organization, and it is also an excellent way to educate and inform members about organizational issues and needs. Governance committees and activities are therefore tools for integration.

In addition to participation in governance, planning exercises are another means to foster integration. For example, a leader may launch a strategic planning process that calls for the involvement of the organization's members in examining the threats and opportunities in the external environment and what actions the organization should take to deal with them. This process might involve off-site retreats, where the members can focus intensively on the organization's future and also come to know their colleagues better. Rather than leading the retreat discussion yourself, you might think about engaging an outside facilitator to orchestrate the process.

Through participation in governance and planning, individual members in a high-talent organization will come to see that their interests are closely aligned with those of the organization. It also allows the organization to fully tap an invaluable resource—the knowledge, experience, and talents of its own members. In the end, governance and strategic planning with the involvement of your colleagues may produce much better results than if you, as the organization's leader, did it all yourself. What you are doing in effect is structuring a "grand bargain" among the organization's membership, a grand bargain that consists of member involvement in the governance of the organization in return for a genuine commitment by individual stars to organizational purposes.

If team members' involvement in both organizational governance and planning is to truly facilitate integration, it must be done according to an agreed-upon set of principles. Such principles as openness of discussion, transparency of deliberations, avoidance of personal attacks, and real participation in decision making will not only make the process efficient but also make clear to members the seriousness of the process in which you are asking them to engage.

If you are a traditional manager, you may be uncomfortable with intensive involvement of the organization's members in governance and strategic planning—the hallowed functions reserved to "top management" in most corporations. While you acknowledge the need for greater integration, you may be tempted to try to achieve it through simulated member participation, through governance committees that have no real responsibilities, and through planning exercises that have no meaning. If that is your inclination, resist it. Smart, talented, rich, and powerful people will detect such charades in an instant. Their participation will cease and your own credibility as a leader will suffer.

2. Make History

A common history is an integrating force in organizations. One of the functions of a leader is to be an organizational historian, to make its members understand and appreciate its history—the challenges faced and met, the temporary defeats that were eventually surmounted, the debt that the present owes to the past. In your internal and external communications, use frequent references to the organization's history as a reminder that it is bigger than the sum of its current members, leading them to understand that they are part of an integrated whole.

Many organizations gain a powerful sense of integration from a distinguished history. Stars' ability to become a team is enhanced by a pride in that history. In many cases, members' status both within and outside the organization and their own sense of self-worth—indeed their very identities—are derived from that history. For example, Goldman Sachs's history not only endowed the firm with a remarkable degree of integration but it also gave those persons who became Goldman Sachs partners special status and distinction in the financial world.

In other organizations with a distinguished history, from the New York Yankees to the Boston Symphony Orchestra, a felt perceived history among the members has also been a powerful force for integration. Wise leaders in high-talent organizations foster that sense of history in a variety of ways, including publishing firm histories, inviting distinguished senior members to address new recruits, displaying historical memorabilia in firm offices, assuring that new members understand the firm's history, and referring to important organizational historical events in their own communications with other members as well as with the public.

Not all organizations have as distinguished and as long a history as Goldman Sachs, the Boston Symphony, or the New York Yankees. A leader in those kinds of organization therefore will not have a long history to help in the task of integration. Nonetheless, any organization, unless it was created today, has some history. It is the task of the leader to know and understand that history, to mine the past, however short, and to learn how it may be used to foster integration. A leader becomes a kind of cheerleader who identifies the successes of the past and interprets their significance for the future.

3. Bridge the Cultural Divide

Differences in cultures tend to isolate individuals and groups from each other. In short, cultural differences create a gap—a divide between persons and organizations. For example, the differing cultures of psychologists and computer engineers in a consulting firm may mean that the two groups of professionals have difficulty communicating with one another, understanding one another, and working collaboratively together. The differences are often profound, finding their roots in their different educational backgrounds and indeed in their very identity as professionals.

An effective leader of leaders needs first to understand the nature of the cultural differences that divide the organization's members and then seek to find ways to bridge that gap. Leaders of organizations with differing cultures must think of themselves as bridge builders. As the English poet Philip Larkin has written, "Always it is by bridges that we live."[4] Accordingly, effective joint action among persons and organizations of differing cultures requires a bridge over the culture gulf. One way to build that bridge is by using culture itself. If culture is indeed the glue that binds together a particular group of people, the creative use of culture among persons of different backgrounds is often a way to link those on opposite sides of the gap. The essence of the technique is to create community with the other side.

> You first need to understand the nature of the cultural differences that divide your organization's members and then seek to find ways to bridge that gap.

A first step is to make explicit the cultural differences that exist within organizations. Put those differences on the table so that the members of the organization can know that differences in perspective and approach are not the product of individual perversion, as some would like to think, but rather of legitimate cultural differences that are supported by different organizational or professional backgrounds of its members. A second step is to formulate a process whereby the members can agree on rules for handling cultural differences within the organization. Here the challenge is to determine how much diversity to allow within the desired degree of integration.

One cannot expect that highly trained professionals will abandon basic attitudes and practices that they consider fundamental to their work. In such situations, organizations might adopt the approach of *subsidiarity* of the European Union in dealing with the different local rules and practices of individual countries while at the same time fostering an integrated single market. *Subsidiarity* means that local rules and laws will be respected so long as they do not interfere with the basic goals of the European Union.

A high-talent organization composed of individuals with different professional backgrounds might adopt a similar approach: The practices of each profession will be mutually respected provided that they do not interfere with the basic purposes of the organization. In short, rather than to consider all internal differences as bad and seek to suppress them, a high-talent organization might adopt an approach of mutual tolerance and allow such differences, provided they do not threaten the organization's basic interests.

In addition to bridging cultural differences, leaders need to think about ways to assure that the organization's new members become familiar with its prevailing culture, that they "learn the ropes." Integration may therefore call for an appropriate program of orientation that might include the designation of someone to act as mentor or advisor to a new member, making sure that the new member is given needed written materials on the firm's background and practices, such as copies of the firm history, procedures, and strategic plan. Such a program may also involve setting up a series of meetings for the new member with various established members so they can become familiar with the organization's culture and its diverse ways of doing things.

4. Become a Communications Engineer

Effective organizational communication is fundamental to integration. Without it, integration cannot take place. Without it, you lead a group of stars but not a team. As leader, you therefore need to focus constantly on tasks of communications within your firm and to develop an ongoing strategy to accomplish them. As leader you need to see yourself as your organization's communication engineer. Not only do you need to focus on your own specific communications—your memos, speeches, and presentations—you also need to think constantly about developing and improving ongoing organizational communication systems, such as internal newsletters, regular memos or e-mails on important events, fixed schedules of meetings that will inform members of important information concerning the organization, and processes by which members can share vital information with each other.

In addition, you need to keep on your own personal agenda your role as leader and house communicator. As you circulate among your colleagues, as you meet with them on their own issues, and as you preside over committees and working groups convened to accomplish specific tasks, you need to keep thinking of how you can use those occasions to transmit important organizational information that will facilitate the process of integration.

Leaders need to be cheerleaders for the organization both inside and outside. You need to proclaim the achievements of individual members so that the entire organization and its supporters will know about them, understand their significance for the organization and for them personally, and take pride in those achievements as a positive reflection on all its members. As we will see in Chapter 10, these activities are also very much a part of another daily task of leadership—representation.

> Leaders need to be cheerleaders for the organization both inside and outside.

5. Co-Opt or Isolate Spoilers

In traditional corporations, CEOs often deal with internal spoilers by firing them. In high-talent organizations, dealing with spoilers is more difficult. For one thing, a leader may not have the legal authority to fire them summarily. For another, even if you have that power, exercising it abruptly can seriously damage the organization. Tenured university professors, partners with large equity stakes in investment banks, politically influential board members, and famous scientists with substantial research funding of their own, cannot easily be dismissed from their jobs by firing them on a Friday afternoon and having a security guard escort them to the door. How then should leaders deal with other leaders who are spoilers? You have two options: Either convert them or isolate them.

Converting a spoiler is not a matter of religious fervor; it is essentially a process of negotiation—a negotiation between the leader and the spoiler. It begins with an understanding by the leader of the spoiler's interests. Once you understand those interests, you can then proceed to discuss with the spoiler ways by which you can help him attain those interests if he helps or at least does not thwart your efforts to integrate the firm more fully.

If you fail to co-opt spoilers, your other strategy is to isolate them in a way that will do the least damage to the organization. Isolation can take many forms, depending on the particular authority that you are granted under the rules of your organization. For example, you might avoid appointing them to various governing committees, remove them if they are already members, and order your public relations office to ignore them.

6. Adopt a Unite-and-Lead Style of Management

Your own style of management can encourage or inhibit the integration of your organization's members. Rather than adopt a divide-and conquer style of management so common in many organizations, a leader of leaders would be better advised to develop a unite-and-lead approach. Rather than diminishing your power within the organization, your proven ability to unite your colleagues—to form an integrated organization, to make stars a team—will serve to empower you in other dealings with them and enhance your influence. A true unite-and-lead style means that you have to demonstrate by both word and deed that you put the interests of the organization above your own.

This may mean that you will have to give up some of the traditional status symbols of leadership. Through your own example, such as by giving up a reserved parking space near the entrance to your building, by using the organization's publicity organs to enhance your colleagues' reputations rather than your own, and by walking the halls frequently instead of barricading yourself in a palatial office throughout the day, you walk the walk of a unite-and-empower style of leadership. Elite followers take no comfort from and do not want a charismatic leader towering above them. Rather, what followers in high-talent organizations expect—and sometimes demand—is that their leader be *primus enter pares*—"first among equals."

Conclusion: Rules for Achieving Integration

In seeking to create integrated circuits within your organization, remember the following rules:

1. Make the common interests of your organization's members apparent through meaningful activity.
2. Ensure that members of your organization understand and appreciate its history.
3. Learn to understand the nature of the cultural differences that divide your organization's members and then seek to find ways to bridge that gap.
4. Focus on the needed processes of communications within your firm and develop an ongoing strategy to accomplish them.

5. Deal directly with other leaders who are spoilers by converting them or isolating them.

6. Demonstrate by both word and deed that you put the interests of the organization above your own.

Notes

1. For example, M. B. Brewer and W. L. Gardner, "Who Is This 'We'?: Levels of Collective Identity and Self Presentations," *Journal of Personality and Social Psychology* 71 (1996), pp. 83–93.

2. H.R. Markus and S. Kitayama, "Culture and the Self: Implications for Cognition, Emotion, and Motivation," *Psychological Review* 98 (1991), pp. 224–253.

3. S. Chen, A.Y. Lee-Chai, and J. A. Bargh, "Relationship Orientation as a Moderator of the Effects of Social Power," *Journal of Personality and Social Psychology* 80 (2001), p. 173.

4. Philip Larkin, "Bridge for the Living," in Anthony Thwaite, ed., *Philip Larkin: Collected Poems* (New York: Farrar Straus Giroux, 1988), pp. 203–204.

CHAPTER 7

TASK NO. 3: MEDIATION

Settling Leadership Conflicts

> I'll tell you what leadership is. It's persuasion and
> conciliation, and education, and patience.
> —DWIGHT D. EISENHOWER

NO MATTER HOW INTEGRATED an organization may be, its individual members are bound to have conflicts with one another. Corporate vice presidents struggle over the size of their budgets. Law firm partners fight over corner offices and their share of partnership profits. Research scientists battle over laboratory space, credit on research reports, and the promotion of junior colleagues. As long as resources like money, space, and credit are limited, competition for them is inevitable. As a result, one finds competition and conflict in various forms throughout all organizations, from top to bottom.

When a conflict is between leaders, the intensity of the dispute often increases substantially. Indeed, it often bears little relation to the size of what is being fought over. A leader's sense of prestige, status, and influence in the organization may become very much a part of a struggle over something that has rather small material importance. Looking back at his days as a Harvard professor, former Secretary of State Henry Kissinger remarked that "academic politics are so bitter because the stakes are so small."

In addition to resources, leadership conflicts within high-talent organizations can also center on nonmaterial issues, such as the right theories, strategies, policies, and procedures that the organization should adopt. Having learned a body of knowledge through painstaking effort, professionals will fight ferociously to defend ideas that they consider basic truths and to destroy concepts they consider heresies. University departments have broken in two from faculty fights over academic theory, governments have ground to a halt because of interdepartmental conflicts over policy, and consulting firms have become paralyzed by struggles over strategy. Even in a symphony orchestra, two musicians can have an ongoing feud when one always wants certain notes to be played short while the other invariably prefers that they be played long.[1]

A certain amount of competition and conflict among professionals in high-talent organizations is productive and can lead to improved performance because it causes individuals to exert increased efforts. Too much conflict, however, can cause a decline in productivity and even lead to organizational paralysis. One of the traditional tasks of a leader is to manage an organization's internal conflicts in order to prevent struggles among its members over their individual interests from threatening the well-being of the organization as a whole.

While leaders in traditional organizations often seek to curtail conflict among members by threats, orders, and even firings, these techniques are usually of little use in high-talent organizations, and are probably not worth much in traditional organizations either. For one thing, both inside and outside of high-talent organizations, leaders may simply not have the authority to compel other leaders to do anything, let alone yield in a fight that they believe affects their vital interests. For another, the goal of any leader in a high-talent organization is to preserve and retain its talent, the organization's most precious resource, rather than to do something that might alienate and ultimately drive it out.

When faced with a potentially destructive conflict in an organization or group, a leader must answer a fundamental question: How do I reduce the negative consequences of this conflict and at the same time enable the contending persons to make a maximum contribution to the organization? Faced with such a situation, leaders of smart, talented, rich, and powerful people need to become mediators.

Leaders as Mediators

Mediation is an age-old conflict resolution technique that can be found in all societies, from African villages to international diplomacy, from urban neighborhoods to legislative corridors. *Mediation* is essentially the intervention of a third person into a dispute in order to help the disputants achieve a voluntary agreement about the matters in conflict.

History offers many examples of seemly intractable conflicts that the parties, left to themselves, could not resolve, but with the assistance of a third person—a mediator—were able to settle. President Theodore Roosevelt mediated an end to the Russo-Japanese War in 1905 and won a Nobel Peace Prize for his efforts. Jimmy Carter in 1979 intervened as a mediator in the dispute between Egypt and Israel and helped the two countries to achieve the Camp David Accords, which formally ended their state of war and opened diplomatic relations between them for the first time. Former Senator George Mitchell spent two years mediating the conflict between Catholics and Protestants in Northern Ireland, ultimately helping them to conclude the Good Friday Agreement of 1998, which laid a foundation for peace in a part of the world that had endured bloody sectarian fighting for many years.

In each of these cases, the mediator was a leader who assisted other leaders to negotiate a voluntary settlement of their conflict. In each case, a mediator helped the parties in dispute to do something that they seemed incapable of doing alone. Depending on the situation, the inability of two nations, two organizations, or two fully mature and competent individuals to solve their conflict by themselves can be attributed to a variety of factors. These include poor communication, high emotions, deep distrust, lack of objectivity, the fear that any conciliatory gesture will be interpreted as weakness, and simply the lack of the skills necessary to negotiate a solution. For all these reasons, two vice presidents, two senior law partners, or two research scientists by themselves may not be able to move toward a resolution of their conflict. Indeed, it often happens that the more they try to solve the problem by talking to each other the more they worsen relations between them and heighten tensions within their organizations.

The entry of a third person—a mediator—into the dispute often moves it toward resolution because the mediator brings to the situation the skills and resources that the parties themselves lack. The mediator's communication skills, objectivity, creativity, stature, and positive relationship with the disputants are some of the key resources that may help settle the conflict.

An organization or group's members quite naturally look to their leaders to resolve internal quarrels that threaten organizational interests. Indeed a continuing state of internal conflict is usually seen as a failure of leadership—a failure of the leader to take the necessary steps to end the conflict threatening the organization. Both within and outside of high-talent organizations, leaders of leaders seek to act as mediators to manage conflicts that may arise among the persons they are supposed to lead. Mediation is one of the daily tasks of leadership.

> A mediator may move a dispute toward resolution by bringing to the situation the skills and resources that the parties themselves lack.

A key question for any leader is, "What exactly am I supposed to do as a mediator?" What actions are you supposed to take to resolve conflict between two squabbling law partners who both want the same corner office, or two quarreling investment bankers who both want to chair the same business development committee? First, your very presence in their dispute is likely to change the nature of the interaction between the two disputants—hopefully for the better. The two squabbling law partners will probably conduct their discussion in a more unemotional, less hostile way than they would if left alone. Indeed, without your presence, they may not want to talk to each other at all.

On the other hand, you need to realize that mediators often fail, as President Bill Clinton did when he attempted to mediate the dispute between Israel and the Palestinians in the last year of his administration. Moreover, mediators can sometimes make the conflict between the parties worse or prolong its existence. Research has shown that energetic third party intervention can be counterproductive in those situations where the disputants are capable of moving toward settlement of their conflict by themselves.[2] Therefore, a first question you should ask when confronted with a conflict among the persons you lead is whether you should become involved at all. Are the parties able to move toward a solution to the conflict by themselves, however painfully? If not, do you have the skills and resources to help resolve the matter as mediator?

To help you answer that last question and better understand how you play the mediator role in your own organization, let's look at a specific conflict that arose between two vice presidents at a communications equipment manufacturer.

Robyn vs. Luis

You are the CEO of a publicly traded manufacturer of communications equipment that has had low, stagnant profits for the past five years. Hired just six months ago, you have been given eighteen months by the firm's chairman to turn the company around and increase profitability. You have been working energetically with the company's vice presidents to develop a plan of action to fix the problem. In order to control costs, you and your vice president for finance, Robyn Kendal, have decided to impose a 5 percent limit on budget increases on all departments next year. Robyn is working with the company's seven other vice presidents to implement the budget cap.

You know that cutting costs alone will not achieve a sustained improvement in profitability. Company productivity must also increase. Luis Molina, the company's vice president for human resources, has proposed to you a new human resource development plan emphasizing employee training and evaluation as a way to improve productivity. Luis's proposed plan is based on the human resources system in the company's Canadian subsidiary, the firm's most profitable unit. You encourage Luis to develop a new human resources model based on the Canada system for the entire company as you head off to begin a two-week tour of company facilities.

Two weeks later, on the day after you return from your trip, Robyn and Luis appear at the door of your office and ask for a meeting. Puzzled, you invite them in. Reminding you of the directive to limit increases, Luis reports that whereas all the other vice presidents have reluctantly agreed to hold budget increases for their departments to 5 percent, Luis has refused and is insisting on an 8 percent increase. Luis argues forcefully that he needs the additional 3 percent, about $500,000 more, in order to implement the human resources development that you and he had previously agreed upon, a plan that he and his staff have been working on nights and weekends to finish. Robyn insists, as she and you had previously agreed, on the need to reduce costs in order to improve company profitability; Luis argues strongly for the necessity of increasing the funding of employee development in order to raise company profits on a sustained basis. As the discussions proceed, Robyn and Luis's emotions rise, with Robyn suggesting that Luis is not a "team player" and Luis telling Robyn not to be so "rigid."

Robyn and Luis have come to you as their leader because they want you to do something about their conflict. These two leaders, while seeking to validate their individual positions and advance their own seemingly divergent interests, do appear to agree on one thing: One of your responsibilities as a leader is to settle conflicts among the people you lead. But before you plunge ahead to judge like Solomon in the way that both Robyn and Luis seem to want you to, you might first step back to consider more deeply this apparently simple situation. With greater reflection you'll see that several factors complicate finding an easy solution.

First of all, any decision you make on the issue of budget increase risks alienating one of these two key vice presidents, persons whose effort and support you will need if you are to achieve long-term profitability for the corporation. You also need to realize that you have contributed to creating this conflict by encouraging Robyn to impose a budget cap and Luis to develop a new personnel plan without communicating clearly to both the need to cut costs *and* increase productivity at the same time. Your own status and prestige as the company's new CEO, six months into the job, may also be affected by how you handle this conflict situation. Other managers will be watching to see how you handle this problem, and they will make judgments about you and the effectiveness of your leadership accordingly.

If you give Luis what he wants, will you doom any effort to impose needed budgetary discipline on the company? If you support Robyn, will you stifle creative efforts to increase productivity? In addition, Robyn and Luis have their own authority, prestige, and leadership at stake because they have pushed their staffs to develop new plans, and because, through tough negotiations, Robyn has succeeded in persuading the other vice presidents to go along with a budget cap in their respective departments. To complicate matters further, you have only a year left to turn the company around. As you consider the situation, you begin to understand that this seemingly simple problem about a 3 percent difference in budgets is not as simple as it first appeared. How do you start to resolve it?[3]

The First Step: Understand Interests

As a leader, your first step is to come to understand the interests of the persons you lead. Both Robyn and Luis have a diverse set of interests in this budget conflict. Robyn, as vice president for finance, is clearly interested in the financial health of the company and the achievement of increased profitability. She also seeks your respect and support and wants you to see her as an important and vital player in your plans to turn the company around. Robyn also has a vital interest in preserving her authority and standing with the other vice presidents and with her staff who have worked to develop this approach to cost containment. If you decide to give Luis what he wants, you may undermine Robyn's status with both groups.

Like Robyn, Luis has professional, organizational, and personal interests at stake in this conflict. As a senior manager, he certainly has an interest in the company's achieving increased profitability and in maintaining your respect and support for him in that position. He also probably believes that the successful implementation of the new human resources plan will bring him professional advancement, increased recognition, and ultimately, improved compensation. An 8 percent increase in budget will bring additional resources to his department and increase his power and influence within the company. Luis also wants to maintain the respect of the other vice presidents and of his own staff, and he certainly feels that an adverse decision in his conflict with Robyn will diminish his standing. This fight is not just about $500,000. It is about the influence and prestige of two of your key vice presidents.

You are not a disinterested bystander in this conflict. As a leader, you also have a variety of interests that you need to delineate and understand clearly. You certainly have an overriding interest in increasing the company's profitability by reducing costs and increasing productivity. Indeed, preserving your position as CEO of the company depends upon it. You are also vitally interested in maintaining the support and loyalty of these two vice presidents, who are both important to your plans to turn the company around. If you grant Luis an 8 percent increase, you risk Robyn's disaffection, the deterioration of what up to now has been a good working relationship, and perhaps eventually the loss of a valued collaborator. If you stick to the 5 percent cap, you retain Robyn's loyalty, but risk losing Luis's. A compromise solution (for example, giving Luis only 6½ percent), may satisfy neither, demoralize both, and demonstrate your weakness to all.

Your Role as Leader-Mediator

Having analyzed the interests of the various parties in this dispute, you next need to think about the role that you should play in trying to resolve it. One possible role is that of judge or arbitrator. The two vice presidents have brought you a problem, have each stated their respective arguments, and have asked for your decision. After all, you are the leader of this organization. Your job is to make tough decisions that will advance the company's interests. So decide!

There are certainly many times when the people you lead will bring a matter to you for a decision, and the best thing you can do is to listen carefully, study the matter, and then make a decision. For example, if Robyn and Luis had a difference of opinion on how to interpret your directive about projects that would be exempt from the 5 percent budget cap and had appeared in your office for clarification, you could proceed to give it. Having heard your decision, your subordinates will walk out of your office and proceed to implement it. But is that the case here?

Your decision on whether to *judge* a dispute or to *mediate* it depends largely on two factors: the nature of the dispute in question and the nature of the parties involved. The issue of whether you decide or mediate a dispute among people you lead depends to a significant extent on how deeply they are invested in the conflict, and on how extensively their interests—personal and professional—are impacted by any decision that you make.

The more an organization allows its members autonomy of action, the more likely it is that a resolution of conflicts will require mediation.

One of the purposes of your conversation with them is not only to understand the facts of the dispute but to make an evaluation of the depth of their feelings and interests about the conflict. In cases where they are deeply invested, your best approach is to try to mediate a solution to the dispute. The more deeply that the parties are invested in the dispute, the more you as leader will need to mediate it and the less likely that an outright decision by you will end it. Similarly, the more an organization allows its members autonomy of action, the more likely it is that a resolution of conflicts among them will require mediation rather than a judgment from you as leader.

What is it that mediators do to settle a conflict between other persons? In general terms, a mediator *helps* the parties resolve their conflict, which in most cases means assisting them to negotiate a solution. A mediator, unlike an arbitrator or a judge, has no power to impose a solution. At the outset, you need to recognize that a single, magic mediation formula does not exist. Different mediators do different things. Theodore Roosevelt, Jimmy Carter, and George Mitchell, all successful mediators, each used different techniques to mediate the disputes they confronted. For one thing, mediators intrude into a conflict to different degrees, depending on the nature of the dispute, the parties, and their own skills, resources, and judgment. In general terms, there are three general areas that a mediator may seek to address: process, communications, and substance. You as a leader-mediator should think about each of these three areas.

Process

At the most basic level, the leader as mediator may simply work to shape a more productive process of interaction between the parties in the dispute, such as Robyn and Luis. For example, recognizing that a sudden meeting in your office after your return from a two-week trip is probably not the most auspicious moment for settling a conflict, you might arrange for the three of you to discuss the issue in an atmosphere more conducive to conflict resolution. The physical site where mediation takes place can have an impact on the conflict dynamic. The site's neutrality, privacy, and security are factors that are conducive to a settlement. It is for this reason that Camp David, the retreat of U.S. Presidents, has been a favored site for conflict mediation.

Bearing in mind the importance of the mediation site and the timing of your intervention, you might for example invite Robyn and Luis to your private club for lunch or drinks, or to return to your office at a more convenient time to share a sandwich. At the same time, ask them to think creatively about ways of solving the problem in the meanwhile and acknowledging your own responsibility in causing this conflict.

One process technique that many mediators use is to *caucus* individually with the disputants in order to learn of their underlying interests and concerns. With their knowledge and before meeting together with Robyn and Luis, you might want to talk them individually about the problem. In a one-on-one session, they may be more frank about their interests and concerns, less confrontational and emotional, and thus give you insights into how best to resolve the conflict. Some research suggests that when hostility between the parties is high, bringing them together too soon may serve to exacerbate the conflict, rather than to begin a process toward resolution.[4]

Another process approach is to explain to them your thinking about the need *both* to reduce costs and improve productivity. While accepting responsibility for not having made your goals clear earlier, ask them to try to find a solution themselves and then to report back to you within a week. You might also gently give them some basic ground rules to follow in their one-on-one strategic conversation. In effect, you are seeking to create a more productive process of discussion between the two vice presidents and then letting them take it from there.

As you help develop a process, you should also work to increase the parties' motivation to solve their problem themselves. You can do this by talking optimistically about the possibilities for resolution, by using your relationship with each one to encourage them to work sincerely to find a solution, and by seeking ways to build trust between them. For example, you might try speaking positively about the important role that each person plays in the organization and the significant contributions that each has made to its success.

Communications

Merely creating a better process may not be enough to settle the conflict. As leader-mediator, you may have to find ways to improve *communications* between contending parties, like your two vice presidents, Robyn and Luis. For example, you may have to help the two sides understand and acknowledge the legitimacy of each other's interests and needs: that Robyn has a legitimate interest in maintaining the confidence of the other vice presidents, that Luis has an interest in increasing productivity, that cutting costs alone will not solve the company's problems. You might seek their advice on criteria to measure results, incentives to make the plan work, and sanctions in case it fails.

One important way by which a mediator can improve communications between the parties is to help them define the precise issues in dispute and to aid them to stay focused on those issues during the discussion. A conflict is often characterized by parties' misperceptions of each other and distortions caused by hostility. By defining the issues, the mediator can move the parties toward active problem solving and away from personal recriminations. More than merely defining the issues, the mediator can facilitate settlement by reframing them in a way that appeals to the interests of both parties. Thus, in the case of Robyn and Luis, the issue is not whether Luis is to receive a 5 percent increase or an 8 percent increase but what budgetary actions can the company take in the next fiscal year to increase profitability.

In addition to reframing issues, another mediator technique is to sequence issues—to develop an agreed-upon agenda as to the order in which the parties will address the issues in dispute. Sometimes you can create momentum toward solution and build confidence between the parties by taking up and resolving the easier issues before addressing the more difficult ones.

Substance

Finally, if the people you lead remain locked in their positions, you might offer *substantive* suggestions as to how the two parties might solve their problem. In Robyn's and Luis's case, you might ask the parties to engage in a brainstorming session to come up with creative solutions that would resolve the conflict by allowing both Robyn and Luis to satisfy their interests.

If Robyn and Luis are unwilling to engage in this exercise and persist in holding fast to their positions, then you as mediator-leader should put forward ideas on possible options and ask for their views on them. Depending on the level of emotion and hostility between the parties, you may wish to hold this discussion in separate meetings with each of the disputants, since they are more likely to be receptive to new ideas and to engage in genuine evaluation of new options in a private session with you alone. In the presence of the other party they may fear that any flexibility will be seen as a weakness to be exploited.

Some suggestions that might emerge with your encouragement could include:

- Transfer to Luis's department two staff members from the company's Canadian subsidiary (i.e., payment in kind).
- Create a special budgetary category for "special projects" or "capital projects" that have to be approved by the CEO and the board and are not considered part of the annual operating budget.
- Tie the continued grant of 8 percent to criteria and penalties for failure to meet them.
- Fund the additional 3 percent from the president's budget, not the basic operating budget.

- Grant an increase for six months, with the additional six months funded only upon presentation of evidence that the plan is achieving productivity.

Mediation Power Tools

In most cases, a leader-mediator is not willing to solve a conflict at any price. "Peace at any price" cannot be the motto of an effective leader because in most cases a leader-mediator has a definite goal in mind: to help resolve the conflict between elite followers in a way that is in the best interests of the organization or group. As a leader, you have a point of view about the conflict and the way it ought to be resolved. If, for example, you believe that Luis's new human resources plan will actually increase employee productivity, you will seek to resolve the plan in a way that will give Luis the resources he needs while protecting Robyn's status and authority as vice president of finance. On the other hand, if you feel that Luis's plan will have no impact on company profitability, then you are likely to want to move in the direction of action that does not give him all that he is asking but will still preserve his morale and your working relationship with him.

In most of the disputes you mediate, you are not truly neutral. You may have a point of view or a definite objective in mind. Absolute neutrality is not essential to effective mediation. Jimmy Carter succeeded in mediating the conflict between the Israelis and the Egyptians at Camp David, despite the fact that Israel and the United States were historically close allies and that the United States had resupplied Israel with arms in its 1973 War with Egypt. What is more important than neutrality is that the two disputants accept you in the role of mediator to help resolve their dispute. Mediator acceptance is more important than mediator neutrality.

> Absolute neutrality is not essential to effective mediation.

In order to achieve your goal of settling the dispute in a way that is in the best interests of your organization, you will have to change the behavior of one or both of the disputants. As a leader of other leaders, you usually do not have the legal authority to order them to change their behavior in a particular way. Even if you did, the consequences of such an order can be extremely negative for your continuing relationship with them, for the organization as a whole, and for your future ability to lead it. However, lack of legal authority or the inadvisability of using it does not mean that you, as a leader of leaders, are without power. Depending on the situation, you may have greater or less social power that you can use to influence the behavior of other persons.

Drawing on the work of social psychologists, one can identify specific bases of social power that a mediator might use in interactions with disputants to change their behavior in desired ways.[5] Six in particular are important: 1) reward, 2) coercion, 3) expertise and information, 4) legitimacy, 5) reference, and 6) coalitions and networks. These six elements are a mediator's power tools. Let's look briefly at how to use them.

1. *Reward.* A mediator uses reward power by offering some positive benefit to one or both of the disputants in return for a desired change of behavior. Part of the United States' effectiveness as an international mediator has been its ability to offer increased aid to disputants who resolve their conflicts, as was the case with the Egypt-Israel peace treaty that resulted from the Camp David mediation conducted by President Jimmy Carter.

By virtue of their positions, leaders have access to resources that they can use to reward disputants. Thus, in dealing with Robyn and Luis, you as CEO may have special funds that you can tap to finance the new human resource plan without forcing Robyn to lift the 5 percent budget cap just for Luis. The risk of granting a reward to disputants in your organization is that others in the organization will view your largesse as weakness, as a reward for bad behavior, or as setting a bad precedent that others may exploit in the future.

2. *Coercion.* Leaders have the power to punish as well as reward,

and mediators have used the threat of punishment as a means to change disputants' behavior. In 1995, when the United States intervened to stop the fighting in Bosnia, Assistant Secretary of State Richard Holbrooke induced the Serbs to accept a settlement by threatening their chief supporter, President Slobodan Milosevic of Yugoslavia, with NATO bombing. You as leader of leaders may also have various means of coercion at your disposal. Like rewards, coercive acts have both costs and benefits. You need to calculate them carefully before moving to coerce a disputant in your organization. Remember that the leaders you lead also have resources that they may decide to employ against you if you become too heavy-handed.

3. *Expertise.* In some cases, a mediator's ability to influence the parties is derived from the mediator's expertise or specialized knowledge. In those situations in which the leader, by virtue of his or her position, is presumed by the disputants to have superior knowledge, the leader-mediator's recommendation as to what the parties should do is supported by the power of expertise. So your statement to Robyn that you have studied Luis's plan carefully, and that you as an experienced corporate officer believe it has an excellent chance of success, draws its force from your expert power.

You need to recognize, of course, that many of the people you lead also exercise expert power in their day-to-day lives. The ability of doctors, lawyers, management consultants, and money managers, to name just a few, to influence their patients and clients is derived from their expertise. As a result, in their own areas of specialization, they may not be willing to accept your recommendations if they decide that your expertise is no greater than theirs.

4. *Legitimacy.* You gain the power of legitimacy from a supposed right to ask someone to do something. As a result of your position as leader of an organization, you

> The extent of your ability to intervene in a dispute between members depends on the legitimate rights you hold as their leader.

have certain rights to make demands on and act toward other organization members in particular ways. Indeed, your ability to intervene in a dispute between members stems from the legitimate rights you hold as their leader. The extent of your legitimacy power will depend on the organization, the situation, and the nature of the dispute in question. While it may be legitimate for you to intervene in a dispute in order to resolve it and to make recommendations, your legitimacy power may not extend to actually directing the disputants to change their behavior toward each other in particular ways.

5. *Reference.* Reference power arises out of your relationship with the person you are trying to influence. It is based on the fact that the target of influence values that relationship with you and therefore will be reluctant to do anything that might damage it. For example, if one of the disputants is someone you hired and mentored over many years, your reference power with that person may be significantly greater than over a person of the same experience level but who had joined the organization a year ago. As we said at the beginning of this book, leadership is fundamentally a relationship between the leader and the persons who follow them. To the extent that you as a leader have developed strong personal relationships with those persons, you gain important tools of influence in times of conflict.

6. *Coalitions and Networks.* In trying to settle a dispute, your own resources may not be enough. You may therefore have to reach out to other persons to help you influence the disputants. Building coalitions and mobilizing existing social networks are important power tools for the mediator to use at the appropriate time.

For example, in trying to settle conflict between senior management consultants in your firm, you as a newly chosen managing partner may have less influence over the disputants than a long-time partner who had actively mentored and aided one or both disputant over the years. By involving that person in helping you resolve the dispute, you are using coalition power to change one or both of the disputant's behavior. Any time you are working to solve a conflict among those you lead, you should always ask a fundamental question: Who else can help me with this task?

Effective leader-mediators rarely use just one of the power tools alone. These tools often need to be used in combination in order to achieve desired results. So in persuading Robyn and Luis or any of the other leaders that you lead to accept a solution to a conflict that they themselves cannot or will not settle, you as a leader-mediator may have to employ a sophisticated mixture of rewards and coercion, reference and legitimacy, as well as expertise and coalitions.

Conclusion: Rules for Mediation

Leaders who are called upon to mediate conflicts between other leaders should remember the following rules:

1. Seek to understand those leaders' underlying interests, not just their stated positions.

2. Consider carefully the process by which you will mediate between the contending leaders and the precise role that you ought to play in that process.

3. Evaluate the way the disputing parties are communicating with one another and seek to improve their processes of communication.

4. Make sure the mediation process and communications are right before you jump in with substantive solutions to the conflict.

5. Consider carefully the six mediation power tools of reward, coercion, expertise, legitimacy, reference, and coalition that you may employ and how they might be applied most effectively in the conflict you are facing.

Notes

1. Henry Mintzberg, "Covert Leadership: Notes on Managing Professionals," *Harvard Business Review* 140 (November–December 1998), p. 144.

2. Dean G. Pruitt and Sung Hee Kim, *Social Conflict: Escalation, Stalemate, and Settlement, 3rd ed.* (New York: McGraw-Hill, 2004), p. 229.

3. A dramatized form of the *Robyn and Luis* case—written, directed, and produced by Jeswald W. Salacuse—is available on video from the Program on Negotiation at Harvard Law School (www.pon.org).

4. Pruitt and Kim, *Social Conflict*, p. 234–235.

5. See, for example, Jeffrey Z. Rubin, "International Mediation in Context," in Bercovitch and Rubin, eds., *Mediation in International Relations: Multiple Approaches to Conflict Management* (New York: St Martin's Press, 1992), pp. 254–256.

Task No. 4: Education

Teaching the Educated

Leadership and learning are indispensable to each other.
—John F. Kennedy[1]

In 1993, the Sri Lanka Securities Commission invited me to visit that island nation off the coast of India to advise it on ways of improving its judges' knowledge about securities and financial law. Sri Lanka was then in the process of developing a stock market, and the government and the Securities Commission considered the courts vital in maintaining the market's integrity. Both the stock market and the laws supporting it were all very new and had been based on American and English models. Most Sri Lanka judges knew nothing about them and had no training in how to understand and apply this arcane area of the legal system.

My host, the chairman of the Sri Lanka Securities Commission, believed it essential to educate them, and he hoped that my visit would lay the foundation for the development of a special training course for all senior judges in the Sri Lankan judiciary. The chairman was a leader undertaking the daunting task of trying to educate other leaders over whom he had absolutely no authority.

Leaders as Managers of the Learning Process

My Sri Lankan host was by no means unique in that respect. Education is one of the daily tasks of any leader. Indeed, the word "educate" is derived from the Latin *educere*, which means to lead forth. Whether an organization's members want to recognize it or not, the job of any leader is to help them learn. Modern management scholars have urged traditional corporations to become "learning organizations," to adapt to rapidly changing business environments, to constantly rethink and reinvent the way they do business. That advice is really not revolutionary. Successful organizations have always engaged in learning, and high-talent organizations are by nature learning organizations. Management consulting companies, law firms, research institutes, universities, investment banks, and symphony orchestras have always recognized that their basic capital is their members' collective knowledge, a wasting asset whose value can only be maintained by the continued and constant learning of its members.

The challenge for leaders of these organizations, given their members' already high level of expertise, is to understand their role in the learning process. In particular, how and what can any leader teach other persons who are usually already highly educated and knowledgeable? How and what is a hospital administrator to teach physicians who are both supremely confident and proud of the learning they possess? How and what is the managing partner of a law firm supposed to teach other partners about practicing law? How and what is a symphony orchestra conductor to teach musicians who through long years of arduous training and practice have come to master their instruments? Just what exactly was the Sri Lankan securities chairman, who was not a lawyer, supposed to teach experienced judges about law?

In short, if you lead smart, talented, rich, and powerful people, what are you supposed to teach them and how can you get them to listen to you? How do you teach persons who are already educated?

Answering those questions begins with an understanding of the nature of education. The goal of education, whether it takes place in a high school classroom or a high-talent organization like an investment bank, is that persons learn. Useful learning can take place in many ways. For many people, the basic model of education is the traditional classroom. The old-fashioned classroom learning model is a simple, one-way process. The teacher imparts knowledge and the students absorb that knowledge as best they can. A lot of what passes for continuing education and corporate in-house training still relies heavily on that model.

In fact, few really good classrooms operate in that fashion. Students in the most effective educational environments learn in many ways: from knowledge conveyed by the teacher, from insights gained from other students, from their own study, from their own research and experimentation, from their observations of the outside world, from discussions and dialogue among students and teacher, from trying to answer questions that they had never asked before, and from trying to apply their knowledge to real or simulated problem situations, to name just a few.

A truly successful teacher understands that students learn in many ways and therefore seeks to manage that learning process in all its complexity to assure that the students maximize real learning from the constantly changing dynamics taking place in a particular learning environment, whether it is a classroom, laboratory, or conference room. Like gifted teachers, leaders of other leaders, in carrying out the daily task of education, need to be managers of the learning process within their organization. The management of learning in organizations and with other leaders, as in classrooms, may require a variety of techniques, depending on the learning problem encountered, the persons taught, and the demands of the organization served. Sometimes, you as leader do the teaching. Sometimes you need to find others to provide the learning.

Diagnosing the Learning Problem

As managers of the learning process, leaders must constantly be alert to the existence of learning problems within their organizations. The process of organizational education usually begins with the recognition by the leadership of a lack of needed learning by some or all members of the organization. You first must identify those situations where optimal performance by the organization or by individual members is hindered by lack of needed knowledge or skills. Once you have detected a problem, you can't develop an effective solution until you have accurately diagnosed fully its causes and its consequences. The chairman of the Sri Lankan Securities Commission realized that the country's judiciary had a learning problem when its judges botched the first few cases to come to court under the new stock market and securities laws.

An organizational learning problem is not always readily apparent. Indeed, its symptoms can often be interpreted in ways that have nothing to do with learning. Like a physician examining a patient, you have to be constantly alert to symptoms, but more importantly you need to understand their causes. In 2002, administrators of a 1700-bed medical center in New Jersey grew increasingly concerned by tensions and conflicts between its patients and its medical staff, as well as between its nurses and doctors. The conflicts between patients and staff were particularly troublesome since they threatened to erode the hospital's patient base and therefore its revenues, as patients looked elsewhere for care.

The hospital was operating in an extremely multicultural environment. Approximately 80 percent of its affiliated doctors were immigrants, primarily from India, Pakistan, Russia, and Africa. Its nursing staff was drawn primarily from Latin America and the Philippines. While its patients were largely Hispanic, they also included a wide range of ethnic groups from throughout the world.

The hospital administration was receiving growing numbers of complaints from patients about insensitive, rude, and in some instances, discriminatory treatment from doctors. The doctors often found it hard to communicate with patients, many of whom didn't speak English and therefore couldn't clearly communicate their symptoms, problems, and feelings. In addition, conflicts within the nursing and support staffs seemed to be increasing.

The perceived tensions between medical staff and patients were merely symptoms of a problem that the hospital was facing. It was up to the hospital leadership to understand the causes and then figure out what to do about them. Different leaders might have interpreted the symptoms in a variety of ways. Tensions in relationships and their resulting negative impact on the delivery of medical services might have been caused by any number of factors—too heavy a work load placed on the staff, ineffective management systems, inadequate staff training, low nursing salary levels that dampened morale, or generally poor working conditions.

After undertaking a needs assessment, the hospital leadership found that the cause of the tensions was none of these. Instead, it concluded that its entire staff, both doctors and nurses, did not have the skills and knowledge to work and communicate in a multicultural environment. Although these doctors and nurses may have had world-class skills for performing heart bypass operations and treating cancer, they lacked the ability to communicate with a multicultural patient population, whose exceptionally diverse backgrounds, cultures, and languages created significant barriers for medical diagnosis and treatment. While the medical staff as individuals each had received excellent medical training in their home countries, no part of their education had specifically dealt with how to communicate and treat persons from other cultures.

Having diagnosed the nature of the problem, the hospital then had to decide what to do about it. As a first step toward a solution, the leadership concluded that it needed to mount a special program conducted by outside experts to teach the entire hospital staff about cultural diversity and the ways of communicating and working in culturally diverse environment. Although organizing seminars and workshops on diversity for the nursing and support staff seemed a relatively simple matter, organizing sessions that the doctors would attend was an entirely different matter. Teaching them, the hospital leadership realized, could be a major challenge. Indeed, when it comes to educating elites, the more highly educated they are, the bigger the challenge it is to teach them.

Know Your Students, but Don't Treat Them Like Students

A first principle for any leader teacher is to know the persons to be taught. Knowing your students is important for two reasons: one concerns *what* you teach and the other affects *how* you teach it. The first is about substance and the second is about process. After completing a needs assessment and consulting with outside experts, the hospital leadership gained a clear idea of the content and goals of a training program: to impart to doctors and staff an understanding of intercultural communication techniques for use in treating people from other cultures. Knowing *how* to teach these techniques effectively to the various professional audiences within the hospital was a much more difficult problem.

Having worked with doctors for many years, the New Jersey medical center's leadership knew their potential audience well enough to realize that physicians would not be an easy group to reach, let alone teach. To ask doctors to assume the role of students would suggest that their education was incomplete and their expertise insufficient. The hospital leadership was keenly aware of this educational problem and so was my host in Sri Lanka.

> A first principle for any leader teacher is to know the persons to be taught; it affects *what* you teach and *how* you teach it.

My visit to Sri Lanka began with a dinner meeting of its Supreme Court judges, to whom I was to talk about securities law and its role creating and supporting vibrant capital markets. The chairman of Sri Lanka's Securities Commission was extremely nervous about the meeting and about what I, an unknown and therefore unpredictable American professor, would do and say. As the time for the dinner approached, the chairman kept reminding me, as if I were one of *his* students, "Now remember, they're not students. They're judges of the Supreme Court. You can't treat them like students!" And of course, he was right. If what I said and how I said it at that dinner had made them feel like "students," as that term is understood in Sri Lanka—rather than Supreme Court judges, which is what they were—then I would have met resistance rather than acceptance to anything I told them.

The relationship between teacher and student in virtually all cultures implies a power relationship, a relationship in which the teacher by virtue of position exerts influence over the student. Smart, talented, rich, and powerful people often resist that relationship because they see it as a diminution of their own power and status, a negation of their education, intelligence, and influence. In their view, those things are their primary assets, so don't expect smart, talented rich and powerful people to give them up easily. Leaders who insist on trying to establish a teacher-student relationship with the people they lead will often meet resistance to what they consider a subordinate role, which in turn translates into resistance to anything they are trying to teach. So if the first rule for any leader who seeks to teach other leaders, is "Know your students," the second rule is the Sri Lankan corollary: "Don't ever treat them like students."

The New Jersey hospital followed both rules in setting up its diversity training for doctors. The hospital leadership realized that trying to put doctors and nurses in the same room at the same time to attend lectures on diversity would fail miserably, since it would suggest that doctors and nurses have a similar status and level of education. The doctors would simply have refused to attend, claiming that they had no time for seminars and that their patients came first. Getting nurses to attend would not be a problem since they were used to receiving periodic training as a condition of their employment. The hospital leadership did not have the same leverage over doctors. It therefore recognized that teaching them about diversity would require a special program for doctors alone.

> If the first rule for teaching other leaders, is "Know your students," the second rule is, "Don't ever treat them like students."

The leadership also understood that any diversity training for doctors would not only have to be separate and special, but that it also had to show respect for both the status and the learning traditions of the medical profession. What this meant, for one thing, is that parachuting an outside expert (who did not hold an M.D.), into the hospital to give lectures to a room full of doctors would be met with resistance, instead of the receptivity that is necessary to real learning. Indeed, that turned out to be the case. As the hospital began to make plans to organize diversity training throughout the medical center, the leaders among the doctors made it known that they were not going to participate. They simply did not have the time to spare. The hospital decided to hold training sessions for all of its other staff members.

As training proceeded with a positive response from nurses, technical staff, and administrators, the hospital leadership began to talk one-on-one with leaders among the doctors about how its physicians might learn to better communicate with their ethnically diverse patients. Through these discussions, the doctors came to recognize that the hospital had a serious communication problem that was complicating and in some cases endangering patient care and treatment. Finally, they arrived at a "medical approach" to the problem: grand rounds.

Hospitals have traditionally conducted periodic grand rounds, a time when affiliated doctors would present and examine particularly difficult medical cases, and when the physicians in attendance would suggest diagnosis and treatment approaches that might be considered. Grand rounds, while never called "training" or "education," were nonetheless important means for doctors to learn. Traditionally, grand rounds were done as a group of doctors moved around the hospital wards, examining patients with particularly difficult medical conditions. Nowadays, grand rounds often take place in a conference room or auditorium.

Through some effective strategic conversations, the New Jersey hospital leaders persuaded the physicians' leadership that a doctor should prepare and present a grand rounds case involving the diagnosis of a non–English-speaking Hispanic patient by an attending physician who did not speak Spanish, an increasingly common phenomenon in the hospital's emergency room. To assist in preparing the case, the hospital administration offered the doctor the opportunity to consult with intercultural communication specialists—the same ones who had been training the nursing and administrative staff.

At the grand rounds session, over lunch, the doctor presented the case, invited and received comments from the other doctors in attendance, and then asked the diversity specialist to comment, which she did. In that setting, the doctors began to learn some of the basic skills of communicating with their ethnically diverse patients. It was through the framework of grand rounds that the hospital leaders created and managed a learning process that taught some valuable skills and ideas to other leaders, without treating them as students.

The case of the hospital in New Jersey and my own experience teaching professionals around the world suggest some other lessons about educating leaders.

Use the Existing Frameworks and Terminology

One important way of not treating leaders as students is to employ leaders' own frameworks and terminology. As the New Jersey case has shown, employing the grand rounds framework to educate doctors proved effective, whereas using a traditional "training course format" would have proved a failure. Similarly, as I found in Sri Lanka, holding a dinner meeting to discuss problems of judicial administration, rather than a seminar to teach judges about securities laws, proved effective precisely because it was a framework that the judges knew and trusted, a framework that did not place them in the role of traditional students. Every group of elites and leaders, whether they are lawyers or doctors or bishops, has its own mechanism for sharing information—for educating themselves. When you educate leaders, you need to identify those frameworks and mechanisms and figure out how to use them for the educational purposes that you as leader want to achieve.

The name you give to the process matters. As we saw, doctors were willing to attend a meeting labeled as "grand rounds," but refused to go anywhere near something that might be called "diversity training." Indeed, in most cases when educating leaders, you should probably avoid the use of the word "training" altogether, since training implies a teacher-student relationship and clearly treats leaders in attendance as students. Terms such as "executive review," "senior management conference," "executive meeting," and "strategic network" serve to elevate the importance of the gathering. It assures persons attending that they are involved in something worthy of their status, and to remove it from being denigrated as just simply training, thereby encouraging other leaders to attend. Of course, if you can also serve food, as was done in the case of the New Jersey doctors and the Sri Lankan judges, that too helps attendance.

> When you educate leaders, you need to identify their frameworks and figure out how to use them for the educational purposes you want to achieve.

One-on-One Education

The role you assume as leader-educator of other leaders can influence your ability in actually teaching them something. Seeking to become the teacher, lecturer, or instructor of other leaders will in most cases generate significant resistance from the persons you are trying to teach. For one thing, that approach raises the problem of your credentials. When faced with a person who claims to have something to teach them, smart, talented, rich, and powerful people, confident of their own abilities, immediately ask what it is that you know that they don't already know. So the question doctors in the New Jersey hospital would have asked, when faced with a "diversity expert" who would lecture them on communicating with patients, is: What can the expert, who has never seen their patients, let alone treated them, tell them about caring for sick people that the doctors don't already know? Similarly, if you are the managing partner of a law firm or investment bank, your fellow partners, whose education and experience may be better than yours, will often resist, if not resent, your lectures to them on law or finance, even though they never tell you that directly.

For another thing, since a teacher-student relationship often implies an asymmetrical power relationship between student and teacher, smart, talented, rich, and powerful people will often view your assumption of a teacher's role with them as a challenge, if not a direct threat to their autonomy—yet another reason to resist you and what you are trying to teach.

Any Oxford don will tell you that the most effective way to teach students is not in a lecture hall but in one-on-one tutorials that are a tradition at that great university. Similarly, one of the most effective means of delivering your message to other leaders is in one-on-one conversations. It is in that setting that you are most likely to achieve the greatest receptivity to your message. First, a one-on-one session acknowledges the equality, individuality, and autonomy of the other leader. Second, because you are communicating with a single person, rather than to a group of persons, you can tailor your message to the needs, attitudes, and concerns of that specific person, and that person alone. Third, through the feedback you receive, you will gain new insights into the other leader's interests and can therefore adjust your presentation accordingly.

Finally, a one-on-one structure instead of a group setting allows you to more easily deal with oppositional coalitions. People in groups tend to form coalitions, subgroups that adopt a common viewpoint or position. That's what the doctors in the New Jersey medical center did initially when they opposed diversity training for physicians. In dealing with other leaders, you always need to be alert to the possibility that some or all of them will form a coalition, either consciously or unconsciously, to oppose a policy, goal, or direction that you are seeking to advance.

More than one new and inexperienced leader has had the unsettling experience of coming up with a new idea for the organization, calling a meeting to present it, and then, as the meeting progresses, watching helplessly as a coalition of the people the leader is supposed to lead begins to form slowly but inexorably in opposition to that brilliant idea. A more experienced leader would have first persuaded key colleagues of the wisdom of the idea in one-on-one sessions before the general meeting took place so as to have a basis for building a coalition in favor of the idea and to prevent the formation of a blocking coalition. Similarly, if you would educate other leaders, particularly members of high-talent organizations, you might think about doing it one member at a time.

Advice and Consent, Not Command and Control

In one-on-one meetings with other leaders, you can assume a variety of roles as an educator. You can lecture. You can give a sermon. You can plead. You can deliver the riot act. Depending on the situation and the person involved, any of these methods of communication may serve to educate. But there are two other roles that you should consider: the role of advisor or the role of client.

Advising is essentially a one-on-one relationship through which one person (the advisor) seeks to help another person (the client) determine a course of action to solve a particular problem. Implicit in the notion of advising is that the problem in question and the precise course of action to be taken remain the decision of the person receiving the advice. Advising respects the autonomy of the person advised. Advisors have many different names: consultants, counselors, guides, coaches, mentors, and assistants, among others.

One of the basic functions of many of the organizations that are the subject of this book—law firms, investment banks, management consultants, medical practices—is to provide advice to other persons. At the same time, advice is an important tool for managing and leading those same organizations. Subordinates influence their boss's decisions through advice, and most boardroom decisions are the product of advice from many sources, both inside and outside the corporation. Even in traditional corporate structures, bosses also know that it is often better to advise employees on a particular course of action, rather than to give them direct orders.

While "advice" from the boss is in some cases merely a disguised command, in many situations, particularly when authority has been broadly delegated within the organization, a manager plays an advisory role. Generally speaking, the more decentralized the operation and the more educated the employees, the more important advice becomes in running a business. To the extent that "command and control" forms of leadership do not work with other leaders, the wise leader of smart, talented, rich, and powerful people seeks to rely on "advice and consent" leadership.[2]

As a method of educating other leaders, advice and consent leadership can operate in two fundamentally different ways: sometimes you, as a leader of leaders, play the role of advisor, and in other circumstances you assume the role of client, the person seeking advice. Whether you assume one role or another depends fundamentally on the willingness of the other person to let you become his or her advisor. That in turn depends on your relationship with the persons you are seeking to lead. Sometimes your position in the organization entitles you to provide advice to its members. Thus, as chairman of an investment bank facing increasing competition from large financial organizations, your advice as to how to confront this new competitive challenge—for example, by transforming your partnership into a corporation and then making an initial public offering of shares—is both ex-

> To the extent that "command and control" leadership does not work with other leaders, seek to rely on "advice and consent" leadership.

pected and considered legitimate by your partners. Of course, like any advice, your views do not bind your partners. They are free to reject them as a way of solving the firm's problem.

In certain other situations, it may be more effective to advance learning with other leaders by asking *them* to advise *you*. Generally, smart, talented, rich, and powerful people like to give advice. They usually believe that they have a rich store of ideas and information and are willing to share them with others, either because they find that another person seeking their advice is flattering to their egos or because through their advice they can influence others. As a leader of other leaders, you can put that instinct to work to advance learning among other leaders when you use it as a means to open a dialogue on a matter that the person from whom you ask advice needs to be educated.

Senator Joseph Biden did just that in the waning days of the Cold War when as a member of the Senate Foreign Relations Committee he was trying to persuade Andrey Gromyko, the Soviet Foreign Minister, to accept certain modifications in an arms control treaty that the United States and the Soviet Union were in the final stages of negotiating. Detecting Gromyko's resistance to any changes, Biden, instead of advocating modifications, took another tack: He asked for Gromoyko's advice. He said: "Mr. Minister, I understand your views, but I have Senate colleagues back home that need to be convinced that this treaty will not harm American security. Perhaps you can give me some advice on how I explain certain of the provisions to them."

As Biden pointed out some of the more problematic provisions, Gromyko responded by telling him the arguments that he should use with other Senators. In each case, Biden responded that, yes, he understood Gromyko completely, but that some of the more difficult senators would respond in this way or that. As the dialogue proceeded, Gromyko said at one point: "Yes, I see what you mean. Perhaps we can modify the language of the treaty in this way to take care of that point." By asking Gromyko to become his advisor, Biden in the end educated Gromyko about the difficulties of ratifying the treaty in the U.S. Senate and thereby secured changes that he needed.[3]

Similarly, in the New Jersey hospital facing severe problems of communicating with a multiethnic population, the process of education began when the leading hospital administrator met with the head of medicine and asked for his advice on how to improve communications between patients and the hospital staff, including the doctors. It was during that conversation that the idea of using grand rounds was suggested. The Sri Lankan chairman launched the process of educating the country's judges about the stock market and securities laws when he met with the chief justice of the Supreme Court and asked for his advice on improving securities law enforcement.

Framing the Problem

Education is the process of learning about something. The effective leader-educator must determine what that something is and then communicate it to the persons to be educated. Any teacher will tell you that how you define your subject matter—how you *frame* it—is the difference between engaging your students and turning them off. Framing is the use of analogy, metaphor, or characterization to define a problem. The Goldman Sachs leadership framed the fundamental question about the firm's future as "What should be our strategy in meeting increasing competition from huge financial firms with a global reach?" rather than "Should we turn ourselves into a corporation and sell our shares to the public?"

For the New Jersey hospital, the question was not framed as "How can we teach doctors to communicate better with a multiethnic population?" but "How can we as a hospital improve our treatment of patients from an increasingly multiethnic population?" For George H.W. Bush, the question posed to other leaders at the time of the 1991 Gulf War was not "How do we drive Saddam Hussein from power?" but "What actions should we take to protect the security of the world and the principle of territorial sovereignty that is the foundation of the international system?"

As a leader of other leaders, you should give careful thought to how you frame the problem that you want to educate others about. First, in order to secure receptivity at least initially, try to frame the problem under discussion in a way that accords with or at least does not threaten the interests of the persons you are trying to educate. That includes avoiding framing the problem in a way that is critical of other persons or blames the problem on them. Consequently for a law firm, posing the question as "How can we get departments in our firm to cooperate with one another more effectively in order better serve our clients?" may be better than "Why do the partners and associates in business transactions have such a hard time working with the lawyers in litigation?" Framing the problem in a way that is threatening to the persons you are trying to educate will only cause them to raise defenses to what you are saying and thus impede real education.

Second, frame the question in such a way that it invites genuine participation and engagement. Real education begins by engaging the other person's mind. The right question can do that. The wrong question can stop education dead in its tracks. So Senator Biden did not frame his question in a way that was critical of the Soviet Union or of Gromyko personally. He did not say, for example, "Why can't you Soviets be more flexible on questions of weapons verification?" That question would have provoked a defensive reaction from Gromyko, not a genuine search for a solution. Asking for Gromyko's advice on how to explain the treaty to other U.S. Senators truly engaged Gromyko's mind in a way that educated him about American concerns and interests.

Never Give a Solo Performance

Good teachers know that education requires the active participation of students. Similarly as a leader who would educate other leaders you need to find ways to actively involve them in the process of education that you are seeking to facilitate. You need to do this for several reasons. First, other leaders, by virtue of their experience and education, individually have valuable knowledge that needs to be tapped and shared to advance the education of the entire group. One of your tasks as leader-educator is to mobilize and exploit that knowledge for the common good and to help diffuse it within the organization.

Second, as every good teacher knows, students understand and retain best those ideas that they themselves have discovered. Education is a process of discovery in which students actively participate. Third, the purpose of education in any organization is not knowledge for knowledge's sake but knowledge to solve problems and improve the organization's performance. The persons you are seeking to educate are more likely to apply their newfound knowledge to the work of the organization if they themselves have been involved actively in its development and discovery than if it is just handed to them. Other leaders will more readily "buy into" and take ownership of new ideas and knowledge if they have actively participated in its development than if they have been isolated from the process and are merely passive recipients of that information.

> One of your basic tools as an educator of other leaders is not the declarative sentence but the question.

What this means is that one of your basic tools as an educator of other leaders is not the declarative sentence but the question. Socrates, one of the greatest of all teachers, developed this approach to a fine art, an approach we know of today as the "Socratic method." The Socratic method's goal is to actively involve the students in the learning process. The question serves as the foundation of that approach because it taps the knowledge of the students, leads them to discover the knowledge for themselves, and convinces them of its applicability to life.

For many leaders, the idea of asking questions of the persons they lead rather than telling them what they need to know is an anathema, the very opposite of what good leadership is about. For them, leaders are supposed to have the answers to problems. They are the font of wisdom. While this approach is questionable in traditional corpora-tions, it is bound to encounter resistance in educating leaders. So the next time you are preparing an elaborate and colorful PowerPoint pre-sentation in order to teach something to the people you lead, ask your-self whether your method is actually the best way to educate them, to implant new ideas and knowledge that will be internalized, retained, and actually acted upon. The ultimate test of good teaching is not whether the professor has delivered a brilliant lecture, but whether the students have actually learned something.

Conclusion: Rules for Educating the Educated

As you go about educating the educated as a leader of leaders, bear the following principles in mind:

1. Think of yourself not only as a teacher, but as a manager of the education process in your organization.

2. Know your students, but don't treat them like students.

3. Adopt the established educational frameworks and methods of the group you are trying to educate.

4. To the maximum extent possible, do your educating one-on-one, rather than in groups.

5. In the face of resistance, assume the role of advisor or client.

6. Pay attention to the way you frame the issue or problem to be studied.

7. Actively involve and invite the contributions of the persons you would educate in the process.

Notes

1. John F. Kennedy, remarks prepared for delivery in Dallas, Novem-ber 22, 1963.

2. See Jeswald W. Salacuse, *The Wise Advisor: What Every Professional Should Know About Consulting and Counseling* (Westport, Conn.: Praeger, 2000).

3. William Ury, *Getting Past No: Negotiating with Difficult People* (New York: Bantam Books, 1991), pp. 61–62.

Task No. 5: Motivation

Moving Other Leaders

> A leader is a dealer in hope.
>
> —Napoleon Bonaparte[1]

AFTER WORKING FOR just under two years as a young associate with a Wall Street law firm, I walked into the managing partner's office one day and told him that I would be resigning in a month to teach law in Africa. The managing partner, a distinguished lawyer with a courtly manner, was surprised at my decision but wished me well in my future activities. As we shook hands at the door of his office, he expressed a desire that all leaders should have about the people they lead: "I wish I had gotten to know what makes you tick."

My old firm's managing partner was not seeking to know all the secrets of my inner life. What he was really saying was that he would have liked to know, much better than he did, the forces that motivated me, the drives that influenced my actions. As an experienced leader of a prestigious New York law firm, he knew that to lead people he needed to understand what motivated them.

The Nature of Motivation

It is one thing for a leader to determine a direction for the organization. It is quite another to cause people to actually move in that direction. Moving people toward a goal, a traditional function of all leaders from national presidents to factory foremen, is the aim of the fifth daily skill of leadership—motivation. *Motivation*, derived from the Latin word "to move," is basically something within persons that incites them to act. Individuals are not robots. They have their own separate wills to action. The task of any leader is to find and apply the means that will trigger—that will incite—other persons to take desired action for the benefit of the organization or group. That trigger is generally called "motivation."

Interest-Based Motivation

The interests and feelings of the persons you lead are at the heart of the motivation challenge. People act when they feel it is in their interests to do so. That belief in the desirability of action may be based on a person's rational calculation of costs and benefits or on emotional factors. The techniques of motivation vary from leader to leader and from situation to situation. Political leaders have traditionally sought to motivate their followers through oratory.

Winston Churchill, through his speeches to the British people during World War II, strengthened their motivation to endure the German bombardments of England and to struggle on to victory. Martin Luther King's ringing words motivated both black and white Americans to fight for civil rights. President Franklin D. Roosevelt's radio fireside chats helped the United States to face the trials of the Great Depression. And, in the aftermath of the terrorist attacks on the World Trade Center on September 11, 2001, New York Mayor Rudolph Giuliani, through his words and actions, provided emotional support to New Yorkers in a time of great tragedy and motivated them to take up normal life again with courage and calm. In times of crisis, people seem instinctively to look to their leaders to motivate them, encourage them, and strengthen them to do the right thing for themselves and for the group.

The task of motivation is by no means the exclusive province of national leaders in times of crisis. Effective leaders in all organizations and groups, large and small, think about it every day. They think about it with respect to motivating particular individuals or entire groups of people within their organizations. The basic question that is constantly on a leader's mind is: How do I motivate the people I lead to act in ways that are in the best interests of the organization?

Management literature and business consultants have sought to answer that question for many years. They have defined a wide variety of "incentives," from bonus plans to flex time, to hopefully motivate employees to work determinedly in the interests of their companies. Like alchemists seeking the secret of turning lead into gold, they have sought to discover the universal motivator.

For the last several decades, one favored incentive for managers has been the stock option, a device that seeks to motivate managers by aligning their financial interests with those of the corporation and its shareholders. According to the motivational theory underlying this incentive, if a corporate manager's financial interests through the stock options owned are tied to the interests of the corporation, that manager will be motivated to work hard to increase the shareholder value and thereby his or her own financial fortunes. Corporate America seems to have viewed the stock option plan as the universal motivator, the one-size-fits-all incentive that achieves the ultimate corporate goal of maximizing shareholder value. While stock options have certainly served to motivate hundred of thousands of employees and executives over the years, they have also led to abuses and manipulation to the detriment of the company, as the Enron and WorldCom cases demonstrate.

Monetary rewards such as stock options are not the only form of incentive that can move people. Other intrinsic and psychic rewards can also be powerful. For example, in 1988, Amnesty International invited Reebok to be a sponsor of its "Human Rights Now! World Tour," featuring musicians Bruce Springsteen, Sting, Peter Gabriel, Tracy Chapman, and many others. The tour visited twenty-three cities on four continents and had the impact of inspiring its own employees. As one commentator noted:

> The event probably didn't sell any shoes. But because the concerts were held at a critical time in Central Europe and in authoritarian regimes of the Third World, they had a huge political impact that inspired the imagination of Reebok employees, suppliers, and franchisees who were engaged in the project. By thrusting the company into the leadership ranks for the global human rights movement, the concerts gave the company's stakeholders a reason to be proud of what they do.[2]

Despite economists' emphasis on the importance of monetary incentives, there is probably no such thing as a universal motivator. Leaders need to shape their approaches to motivation to take account of a variety of factors, most important of which is the nature of the people you are trying to motivate. That is particularly true when it comes to motivating leaders.

Motivating the Person Who Has Everything

Motivating other leaders is a lot like shopping for the person who has everything. Leaders often fail to respond to traditional incentives because they really don't need or want them. The incentive that may move corporate middle managers may have little impact on those who are smarter, more talented, richer, or more powerful. For example, the opportunity of promotion to vice president, senior vice president, or even CEO of a corporation may motivate corporate executives to make prodigious efforts on behalf of their companies, but the prospect of becoming managing partner of a law firm, managing director of a consulting organization, or president of a university will probably move few successful lawyers, management consultants, or tenured professors, persons for whom organizational leadership positions are usually seen as a drudgery, rather than a long desired prize.

Like my former colleague who saw a dean's job as "custodial," many smart and talented people tend to disparage the leadership function, not lust after it. While the threat of being fired may have a big impact on motivating desired behavior in middle managers in many corporations, it would have little effect on obstreperous law firm partners, tenured professors, and managing directors of investment banks. Similarly, in an ordinary business meeting, former GE chairman and CEO Jack Welch might well induce representatives of another corporation to adopt a flexible and friendly stance by saying "Call me Jack," but as we noted earlier that statement had quite the opposite effect on Mario Monti, the European Competition Commissioner.

In seeking to motivate other leaders, the first thing you need to recognize is that they usually do not view their professional activities—whether they are doctors in a hospital, architects in a firm, or violinists in a symphony orchestra—as just a job. It is a profession, a calling, a commitment to an area of endeavor that has necessitated long years of training and practice. In most cases, they view that commitment as lifelong. Moreover, to a significant extent, they derive their identity, social status, and indeed very purpose in life from their position as doctor, lawyer, or violinist.

This conception of their role in life has two important consequences for leading them. First, they often have strong alliances and senses of affiliation with other persons who pursue the same callings. Indeed, that sense of affiliation with fellow professionals may be stronger than their loyalty to the institution that pays them. Thus, lawyers, economists, musicians, and actors may care much more about the opinions of other lawyers, economists, musicians, and actors than they do about the particular firm, university, orchestra, or studio that currently employs them.

> Leaders usually do not view their professional activities as just a job, but as a profession, a calling, a life-long commitment to an area of endeavor.

Second, the traditions of their particular calling may give them a special outlook on the world not shared by other persons and may even lead them to believe that by virtue of their profession they are a special, privileged caste. Indeed, their professional training may have deliberately sought to give them that sense of being special. Thus, law schools emphasize that they are teaching students to "think like lawyers," as if lawyers somehow think not only differently but better than other people, and medical schools are infamous for giving their graduates the belief that they have a status superior to other health-care professionals.

The strong sense of the role, profession, or calling that leaders feel has important implications for motivating them. First, monetary incentives alone may not be significant motivators. Other factors that affect the role they have chosen in life can also be powerful forces. These incentives include associating with persons of the same calling, learning new skills and knowledge related to their field of specialization, recognition of their achievements by their peers or by the public, and career and professional growth. Conversely, actions that they perceive as negatively affecting their professional status may serve to alienate them and cause them to resist and challenge persons who try to lead them.

Different leaders have different motivations for action, and it is your job as a leader of other leaders to figure out what those motivations are. Those differences of motivation reside in the fact that different persons have different interests. It is those interests that, in the words of my former firm's managing partner, "make them tick." For example, as the president of a nonprofit organization, such as a school, museum, or charity, you will find that the members of your governing board have different motivations for serving as board members. Some are committed to the cause that the organization is committed to, such as educating handicapped children, promoting modern art, or aiding the poor. Other board members are primarily motivated by the opportunity to associate with other civic leaders and business leaders. Still others are driven by the public recognition that they gain in their respective communities by serving on a nonprofit board such as yours.

To work with and to lead these board members, as president you need to understand their individual interests if you are going to motivate them to work for the organization and, equally important, to contribute money to it. Thus, an important lesson about motivation is not to assume that the persons you lead have the same interests and will therefore respond in the same way to the same incentives.

And while you are at it, you should also try to determine your own motivation as a leader. What is it that motivates you to accomplish the daily tasks of leadership? The answer to that question may influence the way you go about the job.

One Size Does Not Fit All

As we have seen, motivating other leaders requires you to shape incentives to the particular interests and concerns of the individuals you seek to lead. There is no universal motivator for all leaders. This factor, however, presents an additional challenge for any leader of smart, talented, rich, and powerful people, and it is important to recognize it at the outset: the accusation of unequal treatment. Seeking to find and provide the special incentives that will motivate a particular individual may conflict with the prevailing ethic in most organizations and groups that the leadership should treat all members equally. To what extent do differentiated incentives run the risk that you will be accused of undue favoritism, of playing favorites, and therefore of undermining your legitimacy as a leader of an entire group? That question is real, and you should bear it in mind as you seek to motivate and encourage the smart, talented, rich, and powerful people that you lead.

When I was dean of the Fletcher School, a history professor whom I considered a rising star in her field told me that she had the opportunity to become the editor of her field's most prominent journal, but that to do so she would need significant funding over the next five years to pay for the editorial office that would be moved to the school. When I asked my associate dean for finance to find the funds for the editorial office in the school's already constrained budget, he protested that I was giving a special favor to one faculty member over all the others, and that I would be accused of favoritism. Moreover, if I provided her with funding, other professors would come running to me for money to support all sorts of special projects. I was starting a process that I would regret.

The principle of equality of treatment is a fundamental imperative in any organization, but it may also be used as a bureaucratic defense against needed action. Leaders have to make judgments on the importance of actions that depart from this norm and the reasons that justify them. In this case, I felt special treatment was justified since I believed that funding the editorial office would help the history professor to become a recognized leader in her field, a recognition that would not only benefit her but the school's reputation as well. Moreover, if other faculty members had projects of equal importance, I was prepared to find money for them, even if it meant a budget deficit.

In the end, we found the money to support the journal for five years. The history professor not only did a superlative job as editor of a prestigious journal, but she also went on from there to become the president of an international academic association, while demonstrating in many concrete ways a strong commitment to the mission and programs of the school. As an incentive, the funds for her editorial office were a far more powerful motivator for excellent academic performance that if I had given her the same amount as a salary raise. Moreover, the fears about accusations of unfair favoritism never materialized because the importance of the project was understood and accepted by her colleagues.

An understanding of the interests of the people you lead comes essentially from getting to know those people extremely well, a process that usually requires one-on-one interactions with them. You need to get to know them as persons, not just as associates. That means, to the extent you are able, that you should try to get to know something about their personal lives—their families, their aspirations, their achievements, their experiences, and their disappointments. Here, of course, a leader needs to tread carefully. On the one hand, you want to know as much about the persons you lead as possible, but you must avoid intruding into those areas of their lives that they want to keep private. If you push too hard and too quickly to probe those areas, the persons you lead may become resentful and consider you a busybody, raising defenses against your attempts to get to know them. Getting to know the people you lead is a slow process that requires the investment of a significant amount of leadership time.

On the other hand, you may find, as I have on many occasions, that by virtue of your position as leader, the people you lead feel they need to inform you about calamities in their lives, like divorces, serious illnesses, and troubled children. Like it or not, leaders have to deal with the emotions of the persons they lead. Elite followers' emotions not only affect their ability to do their jobs, but they can also influence positively or negatively the morale of entire organizations. It often falls to leaders to help employees cope with negative emotions and find ways to overcome them.

> Understanding the interests of the people you lead comes from getting to know those people extremely well, as persons, a process that requires one-on-one interactions.

However, smart, talented, rich, and powerful people are often less inclined to seek such emotional support since they fear to do so would reduce their influence and status within the organization.

The managing partner of my old New York law firm, a relatively moderate-size organization, had only the briefest of interactions with me in the two years I worked there. As a result, he never came to know my interests, my motivations, and what made me tick, something that he acknowledged on the day that I left to go to Africa. I had joined the firm after serving with the Peace Corps for two years in Nigeria. On the day that I was hired at the firm, after we had finalized the deal, the same managing partner had said to me, "Sometime, I'd like to hear why you did that?" "Did what?" I asked. "You know, going to Africa." We never had that conversation.

Previous chapters of this book have discussed the importance of one-on-one relationship building in leading leaders. Through those relationships, you gain the knowledge and the influence that facilitates all of the seven tasks of leadership. At the Camp David negotiations between Egypt and Israel in 1979, President Jimmy Carter worked hard to develop strong personal relationships with Egyptian President Anwar Sadat and Israeli Prime Minister Menachem Begin. At one point, the negotiations reached an impasse, and Begin decided to leave Camp David and return to Israel with his delegation.

On the morning of his departure, President Carter went to Begin's cabin and, as a parting gift, gave him photographs personally autographed to each of Begin's grandchildren. When Begin saw the children's names written in Carter's hand, he became emotional, perhaps as he thought about their future in a country that was still at war. Moved, Begin, under Carter's urging, decided to stay and continue negotiations toward what became a peace treaty with Egypt. Carter's gift had made Begin think of the long-term interests of his grandchildren and, by extension, future generations of Israelis. As a result, Carter motivated him to persevere in the search for peace.[3] Carter's ability to motivate another leader came from his relationship with Begin and his knowledge of Begin, not just as an Israeli politician, but also as a person.

As you get to know the people you lead, through conversations in the hall, shared lunches, and drinks after work, you build a relationship with them, a personal connection between them and you. That personal relationship itself becomes a vehicle for motivation. We are usually more willing to do things for people we care about and who seem to care about us than we would for people with whom we have no relationship. Indeed, our loyalties in organizations are generally to the colleagues with whom we have positive relationships, rather than to the abstract and disembodied thing known as "the firm," the "company," or "the institution."

Carter worked very hard to build personal relationships with both Begin and Sadat, and those relationships helped him motivate both leaders to work equally hard to achieve a peace agreement that has proved to be enduring. Lyndon Johnson became master of the Senate because of the network of complicated relationships that he painstakingly built with each of its members over several years. Those relationships gave him the ability to influence and motivate desired actions through individual incentives directed at each of the Senate's one hundred members, persons who were themselves leaders in their own right, so as to achieve the legislative goals that Johnson wanted.

The difficulties of motivating other people have led managers to search for guidance in many other domains. Seeking to find better ways to motivate their people, they have looked for help from religious leaders, athletic coaches, and military officers. The Reverend Billy Graham, Penn State football coach Joe Paterno, and the Gulf War's General Norman Schwarzkopf have each in their time stood as exemplars of motivation to business managers. For leading other leaders, however, sources of guidance on motivation may more profitably be found in politics rather than in religion, sports, or war. The task of leading and motivating persons over whom you have little or no authority is fundamentally a political process, and the example of politicians like Carter and Johnson will be far more helpful to a leader of leaders than those of Graham, Paterno, and Schwarzkopf.

Motivation, Not Manipulation

Much of what passes for advice on motivation in management literature is really about employee manipulation—stratagems to induce workers to produce more, labor longer, and work harder. For example, leaders are urged to find reason to praise employees whenever they meet them or to present them with tokens of appreciation. In practice, as leaders apply these techniques more and more frequently throughout their organizations, the praise and presentations often become matters of pure form and ritual, deprived of significant meaning. Sometimes, incentives are insincere and border on the fraudulent.

Eventually, employees come to recognize manipulation for what it is and either ignore it or react negatively when they realize that their leaders are manipulating them.

In his dealings with Sudanese officials, Egyptian President Anwar Sadat invariably said to them: "You know, my mother was Sudanese." He apparently assumed that his Sudanese connection would motivate them to be well disposed toward him and by extension to Egypt. While it was perfectly true that Sadat's mother was born in the Sudan, over time he came to refine his gambit by stressing his connection to a particular part of the Sudan. So in dealing with a southern Sudanese, he would say that his mother had come from the Southern Sudan. To an official from the western Sudan, he would say that his mother had come from the West, and an eastern Sudanese would hear that Sadat's mother came from the East. Eventually, the origins of Sadat's mother became a standing joke among Sudanese officials. They saw it as an insincere stratagem to manipulate them, and they treated it as such.

Trying to manipulate smart, talented, rich, and powerful people has real dangers since they are usually more capable than most persons of recognizing manipulation for what it is. Your ability to manipulate them is further limited by the fact that they may be smarter than you are and have probably read the same management books that you have. One of the dangers of manipulation is that it may serve to *de*motivate the people you are trying to motivate. Insincere forms of motivation and attempts to manipulate other persons will often result in their behaving in ways that are the opposite of what you desire. In fact, your perceived efforts at manipulation of people you are trying to lead may result in a reduction of their trust in you, thus diminishing your ability to lead. For example, your insincere statements of support or praise meant to motivate other persons may cause them to question the truth and sincerity of your statements on other matters as well.

Convincing Conviction

Your ability to motivate other leaders begins with your own strong belief in the goal you are trying to achieve. As leader of the Senate,

Lyndon Johnson was fond of saying: "What convinces is conviction." As a result, before seeking to convince other persons of the rightness of a particular position, he first worked hard to convince himself.[4] It is important therefore for any leader seeking to motivate other leaders to achieve a level of "convincing conviction," whether it is to build a coalition to go to war or to start a risky new area of practice in a consulting company. The very fact that you demonstrate an energetic and enthusiastic drive toward a particular goal will have the effect of motivating others toward that goal or at least cause them to think seriously about it. On the other hand, your failure to demonstrate convincing conviction will be interpreted by others as your having serious reservations about a proposed course of action and perhaps they should too.

Convincing conviction is reflected not only in your words but also in your actions. By modeling in your own acts the behavior you want others to follow, you motivate them to act in that way. Thus Mayor Rudolph Giuliani's calm courage following the terrorist attacks in New York City on September 11, 2001, motivated New Yorkers to emulate him as they struggled to reestablish normal lives in that city. Giuliani's convincing conviction caused New Yorkers to face the future with courage and confidence.

> Before seeking to convince other persons of the rightness of a particular position, first work hard to convince yourself.

While convincing conviction is an important force for motivation, *how* you convey your conviction to others is equally important. Indeed, you may do it in such a way as to demotivate the people you are trying to motivate. Smart, talented, rich, and powerful people usually have their own strongly held convictions about the future and the world around them. To try to overpower them with your own ideas, without regard to their own thoughts and feelings, is likely to alienate, not motivate them.

While seeking to motivate other leaders through your own strongly held views, you also need to avoid conveying the message that you, as leader, are the primary source of ideas, the principal and perhaps only problem solver, and that if they will just shut up and do as you say the organization or group will prosper. Conveying these messages, intentionally or unintentionally, will in most cases demotivate, not energize the people you are trying to lead.

The president of Harvard University is certainly a leader of smart, talented, rich, and powerful people. When Lawrence Summers, a brilliant economist who had served as U.S. Secretary of the Treasury under President Clinton, was appointed to that position in 2002, he was intent on bringing a series of sweeping changes to that university, including a major expansion of its campus, a revision of the undergraduate curriculum, and establishing the university's preeminence in the sciences.

A man of vast self-confidence, Summers certainly possessed the convincing conviction of a Lyndon Johnson about the ideas he hope to implement at Harvard. But within three years after he took office, he had alienated large and important segments of the campus, largely because of the way he chose to express his conviction. Instead of motivating academic leaders to pursue his goals, Summers had alienated them. His style at faculty meeting and in public forums was one of domination. His critics claimed that he dismissed the views of others, belittled opponents, and squelched dissent. In an interview with *The Guardian*, he was quoted as saying, "You know, sometimes fear does the work of reason."

Summers's leadership style might have achieved results in a centralized and hierarchically structured organization, such as an old-fashioned industrial corporation or a government department like the U.S. Treasury, but it would certainly not be effective in a decentralized institution like Harvard University, which consists of ten schools led by powerful deans and faculty members with lifetime appointments, national reputations in their own right, and large egos. Rather than motivating other leaders to follow his lead, Summers's confrontational style of leadership alienated them from the process of change he hoped to initiate.[5]

Many people, like Summers, grow impatient with the apparent chaos and lack of order in universities, artistic organizations, research institutes, and other organizations composed of smart, talented, and creative people. "Why can't you just tell them what to do?" critics ask." All they need are tough leaders who aren't afraid to tell them what to do." As a leader, you may of course tell your followers anything you wish. The problem is that smart, talented, rich, and powerful people don't have to listen to you if they don't want to. They certainly don't have to obey you.

Several years ago, I invited Judge John R. Brown, a great federal appellate court judge who played a key role in helping to desegregate the American South, to speak at the Southern Methodist University School of Law. After his speech, at an informal luncheon, Judge Brown, a flamboyant and congenial individual, began to talk about the need to reform legal education. At one point, he said, "Why, if I were dean, I'd tell the faculty to. . . ."

"Judge," I gently cut in, "I don't think you understand the nature of the job."

The job of leading other leaders, unlike that of a judge, is not about ordering people to do things. It is about encouraging and guiding them toward a desired end, rather than directing and controlling. It is fundamentally a political process of persuading other persons, building coalitions, and engaging in lengthy, sometimes tedious, dialogue. You need convincing conviction, yes, but you need to express that conviction in ways that respect the autonomy, ideas, and interests of the persons you are trying to lead.

Looking Ahead and Feeding Back

The task of motivating leaders is essentially one of looking ahead and feeding back. Leaders motivate their followers by envisioning a future that will benefit them and communicating that future to them in a convincing way. Leaders are, as Napoleon wrote, "dealers in hope."

Hope, the belief that good things will happen in the future, is a powerful motivator. Although the future is a mystery for all of us and leaders are really no more prescient than anyone else, people in organizations tend to look to their leaders to provide guidance about the future, in effect to make a prediction. Your ability to convince them about the future that lies ahead and the hope for personal and organizational benefits it will bring is an important force for motivating the people you lead to work toward that envisioned future.

However, simply pointing way to that desired future is not enough. You also motivate the persons you lead by showing them how well and how far they are moving toward the desired goal. In management terms, you are providing them *feedback* on their performance. The purpose of feedback is to help the people you lead evaluate their past performance and understand how they may perform better in the future.

> Motivate your followers by envisioning a future that will benefit them and communicating that future to them in a convincing way.

Orchestra leaders, senior law partners, university deans, consulting team leaders, chiefs of surgery, and any number of other leaders of leaders have, as one of their basic functions, to provide feedback on the performance of the persons they lead. Each profession has its own traditions and each organization has its own procedures for accomplishing it, but all look to their leaders to provide or at least orchestrate the feedback process. While the elite follower receiving a leader's feedback may view it as a method of reward and punishment, from the organization's perspective its purpose is to improve performance and enable the organization to attain its goals. It is vitally important that the leader also see it in this perspective.

Conclusion: Rules for Motivation

In order to motivate other leaders, keep in mind the following simple rules:

1. Learn as much as you can about what the person is doing and has done, as well as the interests that are driving that person's actions. Usually the best source of that information is the person in question.

2. On the basis of that knowledge, seek to understand and develop the particular incentives that accord with those interests and may therefore move that person to act in a desired way.

3. In order to provide motivating feedback, arrive at a common understanding with the person you seek to lead of the standards to be applied in evaluating performance.

4. Agree on future goals in the short term, medium term, and long term for that person, and show how those goals relate to those of the organization.

5. Agree on a plan of action that is specific, doable, and clear.

6. To the extent practicable, build into that plan of action incentives that will motivate high performance.

Notes

1. Napoleon Bonaparte, *Maxims 1804-1815*.

2. Craig Smith, "The New Corporate Philanthropy," in *Harvard Review on Corporate Social Responsibility* (Cambridge: Harvard Business School Publishing, 2003), p. 172.

3. Jimmy Carter, *Keeping Faith* (New York: Bantam Books, 1982), p. 399.

4. Robert Caro, *The Years of Lyndon Johnson: Master of the Senate* (New York: Alfred Knopf, 2002).

5. Sara Rimer, "At Harvard, the Bigger Concern of the Faculty Is the President's Management Style," *New York Times*, January 26, 2005, p. A17.

Task No. 6: Representation

Leading Outside the Organization

If I am not for myself, who will be for me?
If I am not for others, what am I?
If not now, when?

—Hillel

At various times in the fifteen years that I spent as dean of two professional schools, as I searched for time to do really important projects, I realized that many of my days were cut up into thirty-minute pieces that I came to call "half-hour ceremonials." A half-hour ceremonial was a meeting, usually arranged by someone else, where I greeted some distinguished visitor—an ambassador, a judge, a government official, or a potential donor—who was visiting the university, usually for the first time, often at the invitation of one of our programs. These meetings usually consisted of an exchange of pleasantries, at the end of which my visitors would move on with whoever was accompanying them to another part of the university that was the real purpose of their visit.

With time, my remembrance of their visits grew dim, and they almost certainly forgot about me. For me, it was not a time when I did "real work," so periodically I tried to reduce the time spent on these "half-hour ceremonials" by delegating them to someone else or even eliminating them all together. Each time I did, my faculty colleagues

169

protested. For them, any visit to the school by a dignitary required a stop at the dean's office. For them, the school needed to be represented, and the person to do that—the most appropriate person—was the dean. And so, the half-hour ceremonials continued for the entire fifteen years.

The Demands of Representation

As my faculty colleagues were aware, perhaps more than I, one of a leader's principal tasks is to represent the organizations and groups that they lead. Organizations and groups need representation because they can only impact the outside world through individuals who act on their behalf—through individuals who *represent* them. Sales executives make contracts as representatives of their companies. Hospital administrators solicit grants for their hospitals. Corporate public relations officers represent their companies by making speeches to civic groups. Receptionists answering phone calls are acting on behalf of their firms. Every day throughout all organizations from top to bottom, its members are engaged in all kinds of representation, some trivial and others far-reaching.

Leaders in every organization have a special role in representing it. Leaders must not only focus their efforts on the people they lead, they must also concentrate enormous attention on the world outside their organizations. A leader's task of representation is not only something that the outside world expects, but it is also something that followers demand. A leader is usually a principal link between the organization and its external environment. As such, leaders negotiate, speak, and act for the people they lead. As *representatives*, they are agents carrying out a variety of tasks on behalf of the persons they lead—seeking bigger budgets, making important deals, securing the promotion of valued associates, and presenting a positive public image. This task not only demands effective negotiation and communication skills, but it also requires leaders to manage the constant tension between the often competing demands of the organization and its external constituencies. In this regard, leaders are often "persons in the middle," who must somehow mediate between the demands of those they lead and the demands of outside world.

Some leaders, by virtue of their public persona, become the embodiment of their organizations. Jack Welch, the dynamic chairman and CEO of General Electric, was seen by many people as the symbol of GE. Richard Branson, the curly-headed, bearded, blond Englishman, has come to represent Virgin Atlantic Airways in the eyes of the public. But in any organization, large or small, famous or little known, representation is always a task of leadership.

> You must not only focus your efforts on the people you lead, but also concentrate enormous attention on the world outside your organization.

While the internal tasks of leadership and the external tasks of representation may appear to be conceptually distinct and some leaders treat them as such, in reality they are very much intertwined. As we shall see, your effectiveness as a representative of other persons can influence your ability to lead them, and your effectiveness as a leader can influence your ability to represent the people you lead. Jack Welch's ability to represent GE to the public was certainly strengthened by the corporation's financial results achieved under his leadership, and his leadership within GE was enhanced by the reputation he attained with the public.

The Functions of Leadership Representation

For any leader, but especially one who leads smart, talented, rich, and powerful people, the task of representation is complex and multidimensional. There are three basic functions that leadership representation serves in the life or an organization or group:

1. Resource acquisition

2. Relationship management

3. Image projection

Let's examine each one briefly.

1. Resource Acquisition

For the members of most organizations, one of the most important functions that leadership representation serves is the acquisition of needed resources. Whether it is investment capital, markets, or human talent, most organizations expect their leaders to play a key role in securing the resources that are vital to its operations. So corporate executives expect their CEOs to negotiate acquisitions of and mergers with other corporations, faculty expect university presidents to raise funds from alumni, and lawyers expect their firm's managing partner to play an active role in the lateral recruitment of lawyers with needed specializations. Although many organizations' members, from salespersons to financial officers, are actively involved in resource acquisition, the organization's leader plays a particularly important role not only in overseeing this vital function but actually becoming engaged in it through acts of representation, particularly when the resource to be acquired is large.

> One of the most important functions that leadership representation serves is the acquisition of needed resources.

2. Relationship Management

All organizations have a dense web of relationships with the outside world, and those relationships are vital in attaining its fundamental objectives. Here too, many persons are involved in building and maintaining those relationships on an ongoing basis. Nonetheless, in all organizations, the leader plays a special role in building and maintaining certain vital relationships with external groups. Thus, university presidents work hard to preserve good working relationships with their state's congressional delegations, managing partners of consulting firms actively cultivate relationships with the CEOs of major corporate clients, and conductors of symphony orchestras nurture relationships with executives at recording companies. Usually, this kind of relationship management requires a one-on-one approach.

3. Image Projection

Through representation, leaders serve to create and project an image of their organization to particular constituencies and to the public in general. Through speeches, public appearances, attendance at conferences, and interviews in the media, a leader projects many messages, conscious and unintended, about the nature of the organization that he or she represents, which together constitute its image. Indeed, some leaders, like Jack Welch and Richard Branson, have such a high profile that their personal image becomes in the eyes of the public the very image of the organizations they represent.

In fact, the leader of an organization is so closely connected to its image that boards of directors in selecting leaders will often consider not only the candidate's talents and abilities but the image of the organization that their very appointment will project to the public. For example, in one search for a university president, many members of the board of trustees of a prestigious university rejected an otherwise excellent candidate because he was then dean of a veterinary school. The trustees were concerned that the appointment of a veterinary school dean, rather than a leader in more traditional "academic" subjects, would diminish the university's reputation for academic excellence.

* * *

The precise boundaries among these three functions are not always clear. The same representational act may involve more than one function. For example, the managing partner of an investment bank who makes a speech to a group of securities analysts is engaged in performing all three functions: relationship building and image projection with the long-term hope of resource acquisition through the new business that the speech hopefully will generate. In order to understand the complexities of leadership representation, let's look at two concrete examples.

A Tale of Two Photos

Bankers, unlike movie stars, rarely attract the attention of paparazzi. Two bankers that did become subjects of news photographers throughout the world were Michel Camdessus, the head of the International Monetary Fund, and Charles Prince, CEO of Citigroup, because of the particular poses they struck in representing their institutions in very special circumstances. Their photos at two critical moments in the history of the organizations they led appeared in major newspapers, magazines, and on television throughout the world.

In 1997, many countries in Asia suffered a severe financial crisis because they lacked the dollars to pay their substantial foreign debts. In order to deal with the crisis, they turned to the International Monetary Fund (IMF) for loans to get them through the crisis. One country that showed great economic growth in the 1990s but had also run up huge foreign obligations was Indonesia, then governed by an autocratic regime headed by President Suharto. The negotiations between the IMF and Indonesia proved to be extremely difficult because the IMF was demanding substantial changes in Indonesia's economic policies that the government was vehemently opposed to. Ultimately, after protracted and often bitter discussions, Indonesia agreed to make the changes that the IMF had demanded in return for a $43 billion bailout.

Because of the size of the financial bailout and the economic and political importance of Indonesia (the world's most populous Muslim country), Michel Camdessus, the IMF's managing director, flew to Jakarta in January 1998, to finalize the deal and be present at the ceremony where President Suharto would formally sign the loan documents. At that ceremony, the news photographers recorded Suharto, seated at a table, head bent over a document that he was in the process of signing, while Camdessus, with his arms crossed, stood over him (see Figure 10-1).

When the photo appeared in newspapers and magazines, the reaction throughout Asia and in many other parts of the world was that

Figure 10-1. International Monetary Fund's managing director Michel Camdessus looking on as Indonesia President Suharto signs the bailout deal in January 1998. Photo: Agus Lolong/Getty Images.

Camdessus was posing as an arrogant conqueror, arms crossed in sat-
isfaction that he had imposed his will on yet another Third World
country. His pose, particularly with his arms crossed over his chest,
was seen as humiliating to Suharto, to Indonesia, and indeed to the
Third World in general. In his defense, Camdessus later explained that
he was simply standing there and didn't know what to do with his
arms so he crossed them as his mother had once advised him as a
child. By then, the damage to the IMF and Camdessus's reputation in
Asia had been done.[1]

In 2004, the Japanese financial authorities discovered that Citigroup's private bank in Japan had engaged in several improper and
illegal transactions over a period of time. It therefore took the draco-
nian step of closing all Citigroup's private banking operations in the
country, a step that would reduce the revenues of the world's largest
bank by $100 million a year. Coming on the heels of other scandals
in Citigroup's far flung operations, the closure of its private banking
business in Japan was a particularly harsh blow that needed a serious
response by the bank's leadership.

In response, Charles Prince, who had been appointed CEO the
previous year and had taken on the task of trying to change the bank's
culture, fired three of the bank's top executives in New York, as well
as several employees in Japan. He then flew to Tokyo to meet with
Japanese authorities, apologize for Citigroup's behavior, and explain
the steps it would take to clean up its act. At a large press conference,
he took responsibility for Citigroup's actions, apologized for the
bank's behavior, and then, in a traditional Japanese act of contrition,
bowed deeply from the waist, eyes fixed on the ground (See Figure
10-2). News photographers captured this unique moment of Prince's
bow of contrition, and it appeared on television and in the press
around the world. As the *New York Times* would comment:

> It was a bow seen round the world, an unusually public
> *mea culpa* by the top executive of a financial giant that

Figure 10-2. Citigroup CEO Charles Prince (right), in a traditional Japanese act of contrition, bows in apology for his company's improper and illegal transactions in Japan. Photo: Yoshikazu Tsuno/Getty Images.

has typically circled its wagons when criticized or preferred closed door resolutions of problems.[2]

Both Camdessus in Indonesia and Prince in Japan were leaders engaged in representing their organizations. Camdessus's crossed-arm pose and Prince's bow from the waist had meaning to the world only because of the institutions they represented, their positions within those organizations, and the situations in which they found themselves. Camdessus standing with arms crossed at a street corner while waiting for a red light and Prince bending at the waist to look for something that had fallen on the floor of his office would both have been totally unremarkable events. Camdessus's crossed-arm pose was an unconscious gesture, an action taken with no consideration by Camdessus or the IMF staff of its possible consequences. Prince's bow, on the other hand, was the subject of extensive debate beforehand among Citigroup's top executives, and it was only after serious thought that Prince swallowed his pride and decided to use the traditional Japanese public bow to express his institution's apology for its actions.[3]

Both actions clearly communicated messages. However, the messages communicated differed, depending on the audience in both cases. While Asia understood Camdessus's crossed-arm pose as an act of arrogance, in western countries, for the most part, it was seen as largely unremarkable at best, or a tempest in an Asian teapot at worst. While the Japanese were impressed by Prince's bow as an act of sincere regret, certain business executives in the West questioned the appropriateness of the leader of the world's biggest bank "groveling" in front a foreign audience. To those executives, it was just not dignified.

Camdessus's presence at the loan signing in Indonesia and Prince's press conference in Japan were in pursuit of all three leadership representation functions: resource acquisition, relationship management, and image projection. Prince's ultimate goal was for Citigroup to acquire the resource of once again entering the Japanese private banking market, but he knew that Citigroup could not do that without repairing its relationship with the Japanese regulatory authorities and rebuilding the bank's image with the Japanese public. Camdessus's goal was for the IMF to secure the "resource" (in IMF terms) of a loan obligation from Indonesia with the necessary policy reforms. His presence at the loan signing was intended to improve the IMF's rocky relationship with the Indonesian government and to show the world his institution's concern for a country in crisis. Despite Camdessus's good intentions, his posture at the signing had the opposite effect within certain circles.

Choosing Your Shots

Leaders have an incessant host of competing demands on their time. One of the questions that any leader must answer constantly is which of the multitude of external demands should they personally devote attention to. Which particular acts of representation should the leader personally conduct and which acts should be left to others in the organization to attend to? Which opportunities for representation should be avoided completely? That was precisely the question I was asking as I struggled to find time in my daily schedule for what I considered "work."

In making that decision, it is important to remember that your failure to deal personally with a representation matter can have negative consequences for resource acquisition, relationship management, and image projection. Thus, Camdessus's failure to attend the signing at all could have delivered a message of lack of concern, which would have had negative consequences for the IMF's relationship with the Indonesian government and its public image.

Three basic criteria can help you decide this important question. The first is the importance of the goal to be achieved through a personal act of representation to the interests and well-being of your organization. The second is the extent to which another person can as effectively carry on the representation as the leader can. And the third is the perception of the concerned external constituents of your failure to personally participate in the expected act of representation.

> Your failure to deal personally with an opportunity for representation can have negative consequences for resource acquisition, relationship management, and image projection.

In the Citigroup case, reentry to the Japanese private banking market was extremely important to both the financial goals and the reputation of Citigroup, and no one but Charles Prince, the bank's CEO, had the status, prestige, and power to assure the Japanese that the bank did indeed regret past improper behavior and was committed to changing its culture. Certainly, if any other Citigroup executive had showed up in Tokyo to make amends, the Japanese would probably have been insulted and would have most certainly have questioned Citigroup's intentions and sincerity.

Similarly, to the extent that you as leader and representative of your organization are seeking to lead smart, talented, and powerful people outside the organization, you may have to devote an inordinate amount of time to the task, since they are precisely the kind of people who assume that your personal attention and care are their due. In addition to your words, your personal attention and care send a clear message to other persons about the importance you attach to the event and to them personally. Certainly, it was George H. W. Bush's personal, one-on-one diplomacy prior to the 1991 Gulf War that helped to influence world leaders to join their countries to the coalition led by the nation that Bush represented.

The Leader's Mandate

In order to represent your organization effectively, you need a *mandate*. You need an authorization—general or specific, formal or informal—from the people you lead that you are empowered to act on their behalf. You also need some means of assuring the people with whom you are dealing that you are indeed acting for the organization you lead, and not just for yourself. If you are engaged in merger negotiations, you need some assurance that your organization will approve the agreements you make. If, like Charles Prince, you are seeking to reenter the Japanese private banking market, you have to be able to assure the Japanese authorities that the reforms you promise will in fact be executed by the organization you represent.

Your mandate is crucial to your ability to lead outside the organization for two important reasons. First, the other side's belief that you have a mandate means that they will deal with you seriously as a representative of the persons you lead. Both the Japanese authorities and the public took Prince seriously because they assumed that he had Citigroup's mandate—that he was indeed speaking for Citigroup and not just for himself. Second, the existence of a mandate gives assurance you will be able to induce your organization to act in conformity with what you have represented to others that it would do.

In dealing with you as a representative, the question in the back of the minds of others is: Will you be able to deliver? Prince could speak with confidence to the Japanese, knowing that he had the power and authority within Citigroup to implement what he and the Japanese authorities had agreed to with respect to Citigroup's operations in Japan. The Japanese were fairly confident that he would be able to deliver what he promised. On the other hand, history is filled with example of leaders with apparently strong mandates who made promises and agreements with others only to find that their followers rejected them later on. Woodrow Wilson attended the Paris Peace Conference in 1919 as a strong president of a victorious country in World War I and played a dominant role in shaping the Treaty of Versailles and the Covenant of the League of Nations; however, the changed political climate in post-war United States caused the Senate to refuse to ratify them.[4] The reason for Wilson's failure was that he had either lost his mandate or had exceeded the one that had been granted to him.

In view of the importance of a mandate to your ability to represent the people you lead, an important question is: How do I get a mandate? The existence of a mandate does not automatically come with the position you hold. Some leaders assume that by virtue or their position and title they are fully empowered to act on behalf of the organization or group that they lead. Your position may give you a mandate to deal with minor matters, such as making a speech on behalf of the organization, but in matters that affect the vital interests of the people you lead you will ordinarily have to obtain that mandate from them and then work hard to preserve it.

As as example, the managing partner of an investment bank will have a mandate to make speeches about its activities by virtue of his position, but will need to obtain a specific mandate from his partners to engage in merger discussions with another bank. Indeed, leaders often assume to their sorrow that their position has given them a broader mandate for representation than they in fact have. This is particularly true in leading smart, talented, rich, and powerful people, who believe they have the ability to defend their own interests and are reluctant to turn that task over to others unless they are sure that they will carry it out in a way that will satisfy those interests. Their trust in the leader to protect their interests is an important factor in influencing them to grant or withhold the necessary mandate to their leader.

A mandate to represent is different from legal authority to carry out a specific task. A leader with a mandate may not have specific legal authority to carry out the action being discussed with an external organization. Nonetheless, both the other side and the leader know that his mandate is sufficiently strong to secure the necessary legal authorizations when the time comes. A powerful CEO who is conducting merger negotiations with another firm may not have specific authorization to carry out a merger. Indeed he law and corporate charter will certainly require approval by both the corporate board of directors and the shareholders. However, by virtue of the CEO's relationships with the persons he leads, both the CEO and the negotiators on the other side know that he can obtain the necessary legal authorization if a deal is made.

To a large extent, your mandate depends not on your position and title but on the nature of your relationships with the people you lead. In this respect, leaders may play a variety of roles. Some leaders are "good soldiers," who merely carry out the orders of the people they represent and rarely go beyond them without first checking with their principals. Other leaders are more like architects, who after gaining a basic idea of interests and aspirations of their followers, set out to design a future through their negotiations with other organizations and firms, confident that they will be able to convince their principals to accept that future when it is revealed to them. Still others are tribal chiefs, who make arrangements and deal with other organizations, knowing that they have the power to convince or threaten their followers to approve. One can find examples of all three styles of representation among successful leaders. But in organizations of smart, talented, rich and powerful people, tribal chieftains are rare.

As in other key tasks of leading leaders, gaining a mandate from the people you lead begins with understanding their interests. As managing partner of a law firm, you may strongly believe that acquiring a firm specializing in intellectual property is essential to building your client base, but unless you understand how that acquisition will impact the interests of your partners, you cannot begin to build a mandate. Once you understand their interests, you need to engage them, often on a one-on-one basis, to think about the future competitive position of the firm and the strategies for facing that competition.

No mandate is permanent. A leader may gain a mandate to represent other persons but lose it in an instant. Those who grant a leader a mandate can take it away just as quickly as they gave it. In the euphoria of victory, President Woodrow Wilson may have had a broad and strong mandate from the American public when he entered the Paris Peace Conference. Within a year, however, the euphoria diminished as the United States considered the postwar world, and then reconsidered and ultimately reduced Wilson's mandate to commit the United States to the League of Nations.

> To a large extent, your mandate depends not on your position and title but on the nature of your relationships with the people you lead.

Therefore, a challenge for any leader is not only to obtain a mandate but to maintain it. You can lose your mandate through your own actions or through the actions and events attributable to others. To maintain your mandate, you must keep your followers informed of what you are doing outside the organization, and involved to a necessary extent in the process of representation.

One of the factors that led to the refusal of the United States Senate to ratify Wilson's work in Paris was that Wilson, a Democrat, had steadfastly refused to include any Republicans on the U.S. delegation that accompanied him to Paris. This slight infuriated the Republicans, who had strongly supported United States involvement in the war. While Wilson did not trust them and thought that their participation in the Peace Conference might allow them to obstruct his broad ambitions for a new postwar world order, their absence would eventually contribute to their successful efforts to block ratification of Wilson's work in Paris.[5]

Their participation in the U.S. delegation would have done at least three things to strengthen Wilson's mandate. First, it would have kept them and their allies informed of the process and therefore served to counter negative allegations and rumors by opponents. Second, the Republicans would have become part of the process and the resulting product, and they therefore would have had less legitimacy to repudiate the Paris agreements. Third, their presence in Paris would have enabled Wilson to stay aware of opposition concerns and plans, thus allowing him to develop his own strategies for countering them. On this point, it is well to remember the words of Lyndon Johnson, a far more savvy and earthier political strategist than Wilson: "It is better to have your opponents inside the tent pissing out than outside the tent pissing in."

Involving the people you lead in representation helps to assure and strengthen your mandate. To a large extent, your followers' perception of the external environment depends on your ability to communicate its reality to them. Their own participation helps to convince them that your reports on the external environment are correct. The presence of Republicans in the U.S. delegation in Paris would have helped to convince them more than Wilson's mere reports that the Treaty of Versailles was the result of hard bargaining with the allies in World War I and not just the product of Wilson's lack of will and strength at the negotiating table.

When Wilson returned from France to find strong opposition in the Senate, he decided to build the necessary mandate by going directly to the American people to convince them of the need to support the agreements that he had made in Paris. He therefore embarked on an exhausting speaking tour across the country, delivering

> No mandate is permanent. Don't take your mandate for granted, and work constantly to preserve and strengthen it.

two and even three speeches a day to enthusiastic crowds. In the end, the tour did permanent damage to his health but did not achieve the end he sought.

Although Wilson's speeches engendered popular enthusiasm for the Treaty of Versailles and the Covenant of the League of Nations, the opposition in the Senate prevailed and the treaties were never ratified. The simple fact was that Wilson needed a mandate from the Senate, not the American people, because it was the Senate, not the American people, who had to ratify the treaties to make Wilson's vision of a postwar order a reality. The lesson here is that a leader must know from whom he needs a mandate in order to accomplish a given act of representation.

Remember that no mandate is permanent. Even though you have obtained a mandate from the people you lead, numerous events may intervene to change those perceptions and weaken or strengthen your mandate to represent them. In the euphoria of the allied victory in World War I, the American public seemed ready to give Wilson a broad mandate to set the foundations for a new postwar era. As that euphoria waned with time and as America faced the domestic issues following the war, Wilson's mandate to achieve his goals weakened and opposition to him grew.

The two lessons of Woodrow Wilson for leading leaders are clear:

1. Don't take your mandate to represent them for granted.
2. Work constantly to preserve and strengthen your mandate.

In representing other leaders on matters that affect their interests, as a leader you have to work constantly through one-on-one interactions to assure yourself that you continue to have their support.

A User's Guide to Representation

Your effectiveness as a leader depends on your understanding what your followers want. Followers expect their leaders to fulfill two fundamental obligations toward them: their duty of *loyalty* and their duty of *care*. What followers expect, if you represent them, is that you will place their interests above your own, and that you will look after those interests carefully.

In the modern era, when "market forces" seem to determine so many issues, the notion of loyalty has a quaint, almost old-fashioned ring. In business and government today, self-interest, not loyalty, seems to be the driving force. Who, after all, serves another out of loyalty? Doctors work hard to heal the sick, but few would say that they are "loyal" to their patients. For international consultants, who often see themselves as "hired guns" in an age of laptop computers and cellular telephones, loyalty to the client may appear to have gone the way of manual typewriters and carbon paper—a quality that once was useful but has now been replaced by something else. Anyway, when it comes to leadership, isn't it the followers who are supposed to be loyal to the leaders, not the other way around?

The Loyal Leader

In representing other persons, leaders always have two sets of interests in mind: their followers' and their own. In any act of representation, there is always a potential conflict of interest. In negotiating a merger, a CEO will be concerned about increasing shareholder value and possibly preserving jobs, but he will also be concerned about his own financial position after the merger. As a result, that CEO may spend more effort negotiating his compensation package than on increasing the payout to shareholders. All followers are aware of this potential conflict of interest, and they worry that their interests will suffer as a result.

In these days of downsizing, plant closings, and large-scale layoffs, employees have generally come to believe that in representing their organizations, leaders always let their own interests prevail over those of their followers. It is perhaps this perception that has most damaged leadership in American corporations. In short, corporate employees and shareholders often consider corporate CEOs to be disloyal.

While corporate shareholders and employees have limited means to defend their interests against self-interested leaders, smart, talented, rich, and powerful people often are more able to assure themselves of their leader's loyalty. For one thing, they do everything they can to make a leader realize that his mandate comes from them, not from a position or title, and that they can withdraw or modify it at any time. So, before leaders embark on important acts of representation, they need to clear it with their elite followers. Whereas the leadership of Daimler-Benz and Chrysler might negotiate a merger quickly and secretly, as they did in 1999, without gaining the approval of other executives, shareholders, or even board members, no managing partner of an investment bank, law firm, or consulting company would dare to undertake similar action without seeking the preliminary approval of key leaders in their organizations.

Second, elite followers seek to assure the loyalty of leaders who represent them by requiring periodic reports of representation, establishing mechanisms for overseeing representation, and for participation in key representational acts, such as mergers, initial public offerings (IPOs), large bank financings, and new public relations campaigns.

The effective leader of leaders understands these concerns and seeks to assure other leaders of his loyalty in representing them. Instead of resisting efforts to oversee and participate in the execution of his representational mandate, the effective leader of leaders seeks to assure them of his loyalty to their interests by consulting with others constantly and by proactively advancing mechanisms that will facilitate their oversight of and participation in the leader's key tasks of representation.

Instead of taking the attitude that you are the boss and representation is none of their business, you will be better off if you recognize at the outset that representation is very much the business of the leaders you lead, especially when their interests are at stake. And because their interests are at stake, you will do a better job of representation if you include them in the process from the outset.

Interest-Based Representation

Whether you are engaged in resource acquisition, relationship management, or image project, the ultimate purpose and result of your representation as a leader of leaders is to advance someone's interests. The fundamental question that you must ask is *whose* interests am I seeking to advance? Many leaders do not consider that question and those that do often facilely respond: "Why, my organization's interests, of course!"

The problem of representing interests is complicated by three factors: one, organizational disunity; two, dysfunctional organizational interests; and three, leadership self-interest. First, often the members of an organization or group may not agree on the precise interests to be pursued through representation. Therefore, you need to ask: To what extent are the people unified with respect to the interests they want you to pursue? To the extent that there is disunity, you will have to engage in extensive internal mediation among diverse interests groups before you effectively pursue those interests through external representation.

Second, the members of the organization may be united in their perception of their desired interests, but the leader may judge that those interests are unrealistic or will not really benefit the organization in the long term. In that case, the leader, in order to be an effective representative of the persons led, will have to seek to transform those interests through discussion and negotiation, often on a one-on-one basis. So a second question you must ask is: To what extent do you accept and seek to pursue the stated objectives of your elite followers and to what extent do you seek to change or transform them?

Finally, all leaders have a dual agenda: their organization's interests and their own personal interests. Often, they confuse the two, either unconsciously or deliberately. To the extent that their acts of representation are driven by their personal interests, rather than by group interests, leaders risk damaging the organization and ultimately their own legitimacy. So a third and final question you need to keep in mind is: To what extent are you pursuing the organization's interests and to what extent are you pursuing your personal interests?

The effective leader of leaders needs to ask these three questions constantly in order to carry out the important leadership task of representation.[6]

Conclusion: Rules for Leadership Representation

Although leadership representation is a complex, multifaceted process, the following simple rules will help you navigate its intricacies.

1. Remember that every act or statement that you make, whether in public or in private, has the potential to affect your organization's relationships with the outside world. Nothing you do is purely personal. As Michel Camdessus learned, a leader is always on stage.

2. Seek to understand the interests of the people you represent.

3. If those interests are diverse and disunited, seek to unify them, or at least build a winning coalition among the persons you lead around a particular set of interests.

4. If those interests are dysfunctional or unrealistic, seek to change or transform them through one-on-one diplomacy and strategic conversations among your followers.

5. Beware of confusing your self-interest with organizational interests.

6. Work to build and maintain a mandate from your followers for your representation. Remember that no mandate is permanent.

Notes

1. *Far Eastern Economic Review*, December 8, 1999.

2. Thomas L. O'Brien and Landon Thomas, Jr., "It's Cleanup Time at Citi," *New York Times*, November 7, 2004, Section 3, p. 1.

3. Todd Zaun, "An Apology May Be Just the Start for Citibank Japan," *New York Times*, December 26, 2004, Section 3, p. 2.

4. See generally, Margaret Macmillan, *Paris 1919: Six Months that Changed the World* (New York: Random House, 2002).

5. Ibid, p. 5.

6. See Joel Cutcher-Gershenfeld and Michael Watkins, "Toward a Theory of Representation in Negotiation," in R.H. Mnookin and Susskind, eds., *Negotiating on Behalf of Others—Advice to Lawyers, Business Executives, Sports Agents, Diplomats, Politicians, and Everybody Else* (Thousand Oaks, Calif.: Sage Publications 1999), pp. 23–51.

TASK NO. 7: TRUST CREATION

Capitalizing Your Leadership

> Trust men and they will be true to you; treat them greatly, and they will show themselves great.
>
> —RALPH WALDO EMERSON[1]

SHORTLY AFTER I BECAME dean of the Southern Methodist University (SMU) Law School, a senior member of the faculty congratulated me on the appointment, saying "I'm glad you're dean, because I trust you." At first I was flattered by his confidence in me, but then I began to think: "Wait a minute! That's it? He's glad I'm dean *just* because he trusts me? Nothing about my vision? My energy? My knowledge of legal education?" He had said nothing about those things, and I don't think he felt they mattered much as far as selecting a dean was concerned. For him, the most important and probably the only thing that qualified me to become dean was that he trusted me. After working in leadership positions over twenty-five years, I have learned that my former colleague was not unique in the way he evaluated leaders. What followers seek above all are leaders that they can trust.

Trust Me

Trust is vital to leadership not just because that is what followers want. It is vital because it is difficult and in most cases impossible to lead persons who don't trust you. Without trust, leaders will not be able to direct, integrate, mediate, educate, motivate, or represent the persons in their organizations. In short, trust is essential to carrying out effectively the daily tasks of leadership that we have discussed in this book. In some situations, leaders can lead—at least for a time— without significant trust of their followers, relying instead on their legal authority, raw power, deception, or control mechanisms designed to secure compliance with their orders.

But trust is essential when you are trying to lead persons, like other leaders and elites, over whom you have little or no authority. In those situations, the reason that you have the power of leadership is that the persons you lead have given it to you. Smart, talented, rich, and powerful people will never give you the power to lead them if they don't trust you. In fact, it is a basic principle of leadership that the less authority you have over the people you lead, the more you will need their trust to lead them.

Trust between leaders and followers is never permanent. Either because of the leader's actions or external circumstances, leaders can lose the trust of their followers rapidly. In those situations, trust just seems to evaporate like water off pavement after a brief sun shower. Many "powerful" CEOs, like Hank Greenberg of AIG and Carly Fiorina of HP, have found that when they lost the trust of their boards of directors, they lost their power of leadership. Sometimes they were forced out the door; sometimes they held on for a time as titular leaders. With trust evaporated, they don't often hang on to their titles for very long either, as President Richard Nixon learned. After winning re-election with a resounding victory in 1972, he was forced to resign as a result of the Watergate scandal less than two years later.

Building and maintaining the trust of the people you lead is an ongoing task of leadership. Not only must you to try to create trust between you and your followers, effective leadership also requires that you build trust *among* your followers. Even if they trust you, you won't really be able to move them toward desired organizational goals unless your followers trust each other. Creating trust as a daily task of leadership therefore has two dimensions: one, developing and maintaining trust between you and your followers, and two, developing and maintaining trust among your followers.

What Is Trust and Why Is It Important?

When my former colleague at SMU said that he trusted me, what exactly did he mean? Why was trust so important to him? An understanding of the nature of trust and its vital role in leadership is important for any leader. Indeed, persons often fail at leadership because they really don't know what trust is and why it matters in what they are trying to do.[2]

Leaders often confuse trust with friendship and affection. We usually trust our friends, so it is natural to think that if you can create a friendly relationship with people you lead, they will trust you. Trust and friendship are two different relationships. All of us have a friend for whom we have great affection but whom we would not trust to manage a large sum of money or take care of a pet when we are away. The law school professor who said he trusted me was not really a friend of mine. We had never had a drink together, played tennis together, or gone to dinner with our wives. Ours was basically a working relationship.

It is important to understand the difference between friendship and trust because many leaders mistakenly set out to become "friendly" with the persons they lead in hope that their actions will automatically result in creating trust, and then they meet disappointment when they fail. No amount of smiling, joke-telling, and friendly daily greetings to the persons you lead will develop trust if at the same time you are firing people arbitrarily and granting salary raises

> Don't confuse trust with friendship. Creating a friendly relationship with people you lead doesn't automatically mean that they will trust you.

based on your personal whims instead of generally understood performance standards.

Uncertainty and vulnerability are at the heart of the trust problem. In social life, the future actions of other persons we encounter are always both uncertain and potentially harmful to our interests. We can never totally control the actions of other people. The risk of injury is ever present in our interactions with other persons.

In theory, when you arrive for work in the morning, the person in the next office may either greet you or kill you. If you are an investment banker on Wall Street and one of your partners is in the next office, you can be fairly certain of receiving a greeting. On the other hand, if you are a Tutsi official in an office full of Hutus at the height of the 1994 genocide in Rwanda, a friendly greeting is less of a certainty.

In the former situation, because of your long-time relationship with your partner and the social context in which you are both living and working, you feel assured that your partner will smile and wave to you as you walk by his office every morning. The risk of harm to your interests, if you consider it at all, is negligible. Although you can never know with absolute certainty what your partner is thinking and planning, you trust your partner not to leap from his desk with a machete as you go by his office in the morning.

In the second situation, knowing the enflamed hostility of the Hutus toward the Tutsi, you determine that any interaction between you and a Hutu presents the risk of physical danger to you. In short, as a Tutsi, you do not trust the Hutus because you believe they threaten your interests, and you act accordingly by not going to the office at all and instead hiding in your home.

Trust is essentially confidence that our given interactions with other persons will not harm our interests. At its base is an evaluation about risk and about expectations concerning the future. By trusting someone, you make yourself vulnerable to harm from their actions. The more you trust a person the more you allow yourself to be exposed to the risk of harm. While you may trust your partner to work hard for the partnership and to give all business opportunities that he finds to the partnership instead of exploiting them personally, you might not trust him, as you might your brother, to manage your estate for your children after you die. In this sense, trusting in someone is similar to making an investment.[3] As with buying 100 shares of stock on the New York Stock Exchange, when you decide to trust someone, you are aware of the risks, but you judge that the probability of gain outweighs the risk of loss. Moreover, just as we are willing to invest more money in some stocks than in others, we feel we can trust some people more than others.

When the law professor said that he trusted me, what he really meant was that he felt that, as dean, I would act to advance his interests, or at least not harm them. He was willing to invest in me. In this regard, he was no different from other persons in evaluating their leaders: They are concerned first and foremost about their interests and how their potential leader's acts will affect them. Despite the hype about group loyalty and leadership charisma as motivating forces for followers, individuals' prime motivation for joining a group or organization is to advance their own interests, and their constant evaluation of those interests directly affects how they will behave in that organization or group.

For followers, every action proposed by a leader has both the potential for benefit and the risk of harm imbedded in it. If followers consider their leaders trustworthy, they will more readily come to believe in their recommendations, values, and visions than if they distrust them. Goldman Sachs' IPO, Woodrow Wilson's League of Nations, and Lyndon Johnson's civil rights legislation would bring benefits, losses, risks, and rewards in varying degrees to many of their followers. Their followers' willingness to support or oppose those proposed measures was a function of how they evaluated the impact of the measures on their interests. That evaluation in turn was influenced by the trust they were willing to place in their leadership. In the end, Goldman Sachs sold its shares to the public and the Senate adopted civil rights legislation because a sufficient number of members in those organizations trusted their leadership. On the other hand, the Senate refused to approve the League of Nations in part because they had lost trust in Woodrow Wilson.

More than just facilitating the task of direction, trust between leaders and followers and among followers can increase organizational effectiveness and productivity. For one thing, it enhances creativity by encouraging members to openly share ideas and information without fearing that the leadership or other members will use those ideas and that information to harm the interests of the individuals providing them. It also facilitates cooperative action for the benefit of the group. Persons who trust each other, whether they are musicians in a chamber group or analysts in a money management firm, are more likely to achieve a higher level of performance—whether it is making beautiful music or insightful investment recommendations—when they cooperate than when they do not.[4]

Trust allows people to focus more intensely on the task at hand, rather than on their troubled and suspicious relationships with one another. And finally, trust in an organization reduces the transaction costs of carrying out its activities. Generally speaking, the less trust that exists in an organization, the more it must devote resources to compliance and monitoring procedures to assure that activities desired by the leadership are carried out.

> Persons who trust each other are more likely to achieve a higher level of performance.

Raising Trust Capital

If trusting someone is like making an investment in that person, trust is therefore a form of capital. Like any entrepreneur starting a business, you as a leader of people have the task of raising and using that capital for the benefit of the organization. Leaders often mistakenly assume that they acquire the capital of trust by virtue of their position and title. You gain the trust of the people you lead not by the fact that you have been appointed managing partner, CEO, or president, but by the fact that each of them individually and in varying degrees is willing to grant it to you.

Trust is also like capital in two other respects. First, it is not permanent. Just as investors in a company's stock will sell out or abandon the investment at any time when they decide future prospects are bad, followers can lose confidence in their leaders and therefore withdraw their trust when they feel their interests are threatened. Although the law professor may have trusted me at the time he said so, he was by no means promising me his trust for all time and in all circumstances. The unspoken implication of his declaration of trust was that my future actions as dean that injured his interests could lose me his trust quickly.

Second, just as a dynamic business always needs new capital for its growth, a leader constantly needs to strengthen and renew the trust of the persons he leads in order to introduce innovations or to overcome new challenges to the organization. Although the law professor may have trusted me to manage the ordinary business of the law school, I would probably have had to work hard to gain his trust in order to undertake a major new program that would have significant implications for his interests, such as opening a night school or establishing a foreign campus.

If trust is like capital held by the people you lead, how do you raise that capital from them so that you can use it to lead them? How do you capitalize your leadership? At the outset, you need to realize that you gain trust only if another person is willing to give it to you freely. No matter the degree of your power and legal authority over the people you are to lead, you can't compel them to give you their trust. They may follow your orders out of fear, but that doesn't mean they trust you. So leaders who declare to their followers "Trust me!" almost never get what they are looking for.

Secondly, trust requires knowledge and information. No one can trust another person until he or she knows something about that person. The law professor said that he trusted me, not because I held the title of dean, but because he and I had worked together as colleagues for two years during which we came to know and evaluate one another.

A first step in seeking to gain the trust of the people you lead is to let them get to know you in a way that allows them to evaluate your intentions and the impact that you may have on their interests. So at SMU, I could assume a certain level trust from the faculty and staff because they had known me as a colleague for two years, but when I became dean of the Fletcher School of Law and Diplomacy at Tufts University I did not assume that same level of trust existed because no one at Fletcher had worked with me before.

The tasks of trust building at the two institutions were therefore very different. At Fletcher, I spent the first several months of my deanship in long, one-on-one meetings with faculty, staff, and student representatives, and I avoided suggesting any significant initiatives until I felt I knew the place thoroughly. At SMU, because I knew the community and they knew me, I started a strategic planning process in the second month. New leaders often feel that when they arrive on the scene, they need to announce major new directions in order to assert their leadership. If you have that impulse, restrain it. It will only generate distrust among people who don't yet know you.

The precise knowledge about you that your followers are seeking is information that will allow them to make predictions about your future actions with respect to their interests. What this means is that they are not just seeking to learn about your golf game or your college exploits, but about your capabilities, intentions, and values as they may affect them. One of the important ways you can convey these factors is not just through your own declarations but equally important by getting to know the people you lead.

Several years ago, a law school in Pennsylvania asked me to help mediate the troubled relationship between its faculty and its dean, who had been appointed two years previously. The faculty did not trust the dean, and the dean, who had had a successful tenure at another institution, was mystified as to the reasons why. As I met individually with faculty members to discuss the problem, I kept hearing the same theme: "The dean doesn't know us." As conversations proceeded, I also came to realize something else: the faculty didn't know the dean.

An experienced law school administrator, the dean had arrived at the law school in Pennsylvania and had immediately plunged into the task of managing its affairs, letting the faculty, who after all had played a key role in selecting him, get on with the job of teaching students and doing legal research. The faculty's lack of knowledge about the new dean and his intentions, as well as the dean's own apparent ignorance of their interests, led to their increasing distrust of the dean. "What exactly is going on in the dean's office?" became the daily question among the school's professors. It was both a question and a statement of distrust.

By not coming to know the faculty, the dean created a strong reason for distrusting him. In effect, the faculty was saying, if the dean doesn't know us and our concerns, how can he lead this school in a way that will meet our interests? Indeed, he must not care about our interests, so how can we trust him? A relationship of trust between two persons requires mutual knowledge. In order to begin the process of gaining mutual knowledge and thereby building a relationship of trust between the dean and the faculty, we organized a two-day retreat in the Pennsylvania countryside where they could talk freely about their hopes, fears, intentions, and concerns for their law school. Ultimately, the dean and the faculty would gain the mutual knowledge, understanding, and eventually, the trust needed for an effective working relationship, and the dean continued to serve in that position for many years.

Openness

Beyond just exchanging information, the dean needed to develop a different approach to working with the faculty. In particular, he needed to become more open in his approach to leading the law school. If mutual information is the first foundation stone of trust, openness is the second. Openness in a leader is not just an easy smile, a charming manner, and a ready handshake. Openness in a leader refers to the process by which he or she makes decisions, for it is decisions—not smiles and handshakes—that have implications for followers' interests.

Openness in a leader's style has many dimensions. First, it means sharing information with the people you lead. Many leaders excel at playing "hide the ball"—by manipulating, distorting, and selectively rationing the information that they give to their followers. While that approach may enable you to achieve certain results, it will not gain you the trust of those you lead, particularly of other leaders. Smart, talented, rich, and powerful people can readily discern when they have been provided partial or distorted information, and they will readily interpret it as your lack of confidence in them, a situation that will not engender trust in you. After all, if you don't trust them, why should they trust you?

Openness also means a willingness to involve your followers in the decisions that you make on their behalf. One cause of distrust between the Pennsylvania law school dean and the faculty was the fact that he had made decisions affecting their interests without consulting them. If trust arises from a feeling of confidence about predicting the future behavior of another person, that confidence increases when that person involves others in decision-making processes rather than excludes them. The dean therefore needed to change his approach to leading the smart and talented people on his faculty by creating mechanisms such as committees, faculty retreats, and one-on-one consultations to involve the faculty in helping to arrive at leadership decisions affecting their interests. He gained their trust by sharing control of the school with them, a technique that all leaders should consider, particularly in seeking to lead other leaders.

> Openness is not just an easy smile or a charming manner; it refers to the process by which you make decisions that have implications for your followers' interests.

Openness not only helps to create trust; it also facilitates maintaining it. By being open in making a decision through consultation with and transparency toward the people you lead, you encourage them to continue their trust and hopefully to raise it to higher levels. In dealing with the Soviet Union on arms control, President Ronald Reagan quoted a Russian proverb to the Soviet leader Mikael Gorbachev: "Trust but verify." Some critics interpreted that statement as "We don't trust you." What that proverb also means is that our trust will continue into the future to the extent that we can ascertain that you are living up to your commitments in the present. So to maintain and develop trust, it is important for leaders to show their followers constantly that they have actually done what they have promised to do.

Trust by Increments

Trust in a leader does not just spring full-blown into existence the way Athena sprang from the head of Zeus. Instead, followers' trust in their leaders grows one small step at a time. It evolves by increments. Over time, with increasing knowledge of and experience with each other, and more evidence that the leader is open to his followers, involves them in decision making, and actually delivers on his promises, followers increase their level of trust in their leaders.

In international relations, when dealing with adversaries, there is the concept of "confidence building measures," which means that each side to a previous hostility takes a series of small steps in order to show the other side their peaceful intentions, thereby over time developing a relationship of increasing trust. New leaders seeking to build trust should adopt the same approach in dealing with their new constituents. By planning out a series of small actions in their followers' interests on which they can deliver, they lay the basis of increasing trust. Like an entrepreneur who gains small amounts of capital from an investor and then obtains larger and larger investments as the business demonstrates success, a leader also obtains growing trust by in-crements from followers.

Trust First

In organizations, leaders can often begin the process of creating trust by trusting first—by taking actions that show their trust in the people they are trying to lead. Usually, by trusting first, you make yourself vulnerable to the unpredictable and potentially harmful responses of other persons. When the Pennsylvania law school dean agreed to par-ticipate in a two-day retreat with his faculty, his participation was an act of trust in the faculty. He was trusting that the faculty would genu-inely use the retreat as an opportunity to improve relationships within the school and not simply to denounce him for his real and imagined errors over the previous two years.

Recognizing his vulnerability, the faculty at the retreat responded by engaging in a dialogue that was both constructive, in the sense that it avoided personal attacks on the dean, and open, in the sense that the faculty expressed their genuine concerns and aspirations. The con-structive tenor of the conversation was a response to the dean's own willingness to participate. The openness of their comments, which in turn could have rendered them potentially vulnerable to retribution from the dean on their return to the school, was the faculty's respon-sive act of trust in the dean.

The need for the leader to trust first is another way that gaining trust is like raising capital. Normally, you can't raise capital from other investors unless you yourself have first invested some of your own money in the business.

Get Them to Trust One Another

Some leaders avidly seek the trust of their followers while at the same time actively discouraging them from trusting each other; they fear that followers who trust each other too much will threaten their lead-ership. I once worked for a university president, a creative and dynamic leader, who discouraged the university's deans from meeting together when he was not present. He considered too much cooperation as a threat his leadership, so he practiced the age-old strategy of divide and conquer. Leaders following this strategy pit one associate against another; they selectively provide information to one group in the organization and not another; they play favorites. While divide-and-conquer leadership has indeed sometimes brought positive results to many of its practitioners, like my former president, one may ask whether the creation of a more positive climate of trust might not have enhanced organizational effectiveness in the long run.

It is extremely difficult for you as leader to gain the trust of other leaders if you do not at the same time seek to increase trust among them. Divide-and-conquer leadership heightens members' sense of their own vulnerability and increases their need to be defensive in all their interactions—factors that inhibit trust generally. Divide-and-conquer is unpredictable by nature. Unpredictability increases members' sense of vulnerability with respect to your actions and therefore inhibits their trust in you. So if you want to gain the trust of your followers, you need to find ways to encourage them to trust each other.

Developing trust among the people you lead is also an incremental process. They will not trust each other because you order them to any more than they will trust you because you say so. Your followers will learn to trust one another through experiences of working together that they judge to have advanced or at least not injured their interests, experiences that give them the knowledge of one another and confidence in the future actions of one other. One significant approach is to develop joint activities (such as organizational planning and implementation exercises) to give them the experience of working together and hopefully achieve the positive results that will lead to increased trust.

Joint Training

Another approach is joint training. The interaction that accompanies learning together can heighten trust in a group. Toward the end of the apartheid era in South Africa, international agencies organized joint training sessions in negotiation in which black and white South African leaders participated together. The experience of engaging in interactive training was a first step in building trust among the contending groups, for it enabled them to know one another personally, to develop a common vocabulary to communicate with one another, and to learn basic skills of relating to one another.

The trust that began in these sessions helped to foster the final negotiations that brought a peaceful end to apartheid and the transition to a black majority government. Leaders seeking to foster cooperation among the smart, talented, rich and powerful people that they lead can use similar techniques such as planning retreats, training sessions, simulated exercises, and implementation activities that deliberately seek to bring together people who have not previously had significant experience working together.

Obstacles to Trust

Creating trust is not just a matter of a leader's good intentions. In the course of a leadership journey, a leader, like a white-water canoeist, must navigate to avoid numerous obstacles, both apparent and hidden, that threaten to prevent the development of trust or destroy the trust that exists. Here are a few of the obstacles to which every leader should be alert.

1. *Lack of Time.* Building trust takes time. The pressure to achieve organizational results rapidly through sudden changes and innovations when a new leader arrives on the scene often increases distrust. When possible, leaders should seek to lay the foundation of trust before introducing sweeping change.

2. *The Perceived Untrustworthy Act.* Psychological research clearly shows that actions by a leader, regardless of good intentions, that followers perceive as untrustworthy serve to undermine the development of trust.[5] In making decisions, leaders need to ask: How will my followers perceive my action? Often, they may interpret a leader's inconsistent acts as evidence of untrustworthiness. While one perceived untrustworthy act will not permanently prevent the development of trust with the people you lead, you will have to work hard and persistently to overcome its effects.

3. *An Overly Competitive Environment.* An overly competitive environment within organizations (a phenomenon often fostered by leaders as a means to increase productivity and motivate followers) can also serve to undermine trust. In an overly competitive environment, members of the group view each other as threats to their individual interests and therefore have a disincentive to trust one another. The challenge for any leader is to foster trust and cooperation and at the same time find ways to encourage each member to make a maximum contribution to the organization.

A client of mine, a new leader seeking to increase productivity of his organization, complained, "There is just too much cooperation around here. The employees keep talking about how they are a 'family.' I don't want them to be a family. I want them to be a team." "What's the difference?" I asked. "The prodigal son!" he shot back. What he meant was that in the cooperative and trusting atmosphere of a family, its members accept each other's failings, often without complaint, whereas team members expect and indeed demand high performance from one another. In his view, for purposes of increasing productivity, a team struck a better balance between cooperation and competition than did a family.

4. *Leadership Mobility.* Trust is personal. Followers develop trust in the leader's person, not the position or title. Because trust creation takes time, frequent changes of leadership in organizations, so common in contemporary American institutions, tend to inhibit the devel-

opment of trust. Each time a new leader arrives on the scene, the process of trust creation must begin anew. Moreover, knowing that a new leader will probably not stay long on the job, members may see little point in investing the time and effort in developing working relationships characterized by a high degree of trust.

5. *The Exaggerated Leadership Ego.* All of us have egos, and all of us—leaders and followers—pursue our own interests. While recognizing these facts, followers also demand leaders who will at the same time work to advance followers' interests—as we have repeatedly emphasized in this book. It is only when they are certain of a leader's intentions in this regard that they are willing to grant their trust. Individuals who assume positions of leadership can manifest their egos in extreme and exaggerated ways, from the language they speak to the people they surround themselves with, from the way they decorate their offices to the way they treat subordinates. These exaggerated manifestations of leadership ego can become an obstacle to trust because they carry a strong message: "My interests come first—before your interests and before the institution's."

While the so-called charismatic leader has been considered important to many organizations, the line between charisma and egomania has not always been clear. There is reason to believe that charismatic leaders tend to extreme narcissism, causing them to promote projects like mergers to expand their empires without increasing their organization's profitability, which serve their personal interests rather than those of the organization.[6] Smart, talented, rich, and powerful people tend to be particularly skeptical of the charismatic leader and the exaggerated leadership ego, if only because they both offend the basic notion of *primes inter pares*, first among equals, that for them is the fundamental principle that makes them willing to follow other leaders.

Conclusion: Rules of Trust

In seeking to gain the trust of other leaders so you can lead them, you should bear in mind a few simple rules that emerge from our discussion.

1. Recognize that people will trust you not because of your charisma, your charm, or your vision, but because they have concluded that your leadership will advance their interests. You therefore need to work to understand the people you lead and to know their interests.

2. Trust building takes time, so be prepared to invest the necessary time in the process.

3. Find ways to demonstrate that your interests are the same as your followers.

4. To gain the trust of others, you must trust first.

5. Trust building proceeds by increments. So have a plan for a sequence of trust building measures.

6. The provision of information and your openness to those you lead are important building blocks of trust.

7. Be consistent and predictable in your actions as leader. Beware of the trust obstacles of lack of time, leadership mobility, an overly competitive environment, and exaggerated manifestations of the leadership ego.

Notes

1. Ralph Waldo Emerson, *Essays, First Series: Prudence* (Cambridge, Mass.: Belknap Press of Harvard University Press, 1979).

2. Dale E. Zand, *The Leadership Triad: Knowledge, Trust and Power* (New York: Oxford University Press, 1997).

3. Niklas Luhman, *Trust and Power* (New York: John Wiley & Sons, 1979).

4. Gilbert W. Fairholm, *Leadership and the Culture of Trust* (Westport, Conn.: Praeger, 1994).

5. Robert Axelrod, *The Complexity of Cooperation: Agent-Based Models of Competition and Collaboration* (Princeton: Princeton University Press, 1997).

6. Yassin Sankar, "Character Not Charisma Is the Critical Measure of Leadership Excellence," *Journal of Leadership and Organization Studies* 9, 4 (2003), p. 47.

FURTHER READING ON LEADERSHIP

FOR OTHER THOUGHTS and perspectives on leadership, you may want to consult the following books:

Adair, John. *The Skills of Leadership*. Toronto, Canada: Fitzhenry & Whiteside, 1984.

Burns, James MacGregor. *Leadership*. New York: Harper & Row, 1979.

Fairholm, Gilbert W. *Leadership and the Culture of Trust*. Westport, Conn.: Praeger Publishers, 1994.

Galford, Robert M. *The Trusted Leader: Bringing Out the Best in Your People and Your Company*. New York: Free Press, 2002.

Gergen, David. *Eyewitness to Power: The Essence of Leadership, Nixon to Clinton*. New York: Simon and Schuster, 2000.

Giuliani, Rudolph W., and Ken Kurson. *Leadership*. New York: Hyperion, 2002.

Glen, Paul. *Leading Geeks: How to Manage and Lead People Who Deliver Technology*. San Francisco: Jossey-Bass, 2003.

Harrell, Keith, ed., *The Attitude of Leadership: Taking the Lead and Keeping It*. Hoboken, N.J.: John Wiley and Sons, Inc., 2003.

Hayward, Sue. *Women Leading*. New York: Palgrave Macmillan, 2005.

Heller, Frank A. *Managerial Decision-Making: A Study of Leadership Styles and Power-Sharing Among Senior Managers*. Assen, Netherlands: Van Gorcum, 1971.

Horton, Thomas R. *The CEO Paradox: The Privilege and Accountability of Leadership*. New York: AMACOM, 1992.

Israel, Fred L., ed. *Taught to Lead: the Education of the Presidents of the United States*. Philadelphia: Mason Crest, 2004.

Kellerman, Barbara. *Bad Leadership: What It Is, How It Happens, Why It Matters*. Boston, Mass.: Harvard Business School Press, 2004.

Lord, Carnes. *The Modern Prince: What Leaders Need to Know Now*. New Haven, Conn.: Yale University Press, 2003.

Luhmann, Niklas. *Trust and Power*. Chichester, U.K.: John Wiley & Sons, 1979.

O'Toole, James. *Leadership A to Z: A Guide for the Appropriately Ambitious*. San Francisco: Jossey-Bass, 1999.

Perkins, Dennis N.T., et al., *Leading at the Edge: Leadership Lessons from Shackleton's Antarctic Expedition*. New York: AMACOM, 2000.

Preston, Thomas. *The President and His Inner Circle: Leadership Style and the Advisory Process in Foreign Affairs*. New York: Columbia University Press, 2001.

Woodward, Bob. *Bush at War*. New York: Simon and Schuster, 2002.

Yukl, Gary. *Leadership in Organizations*. Upper Saddle River, N.J.: Prentice Hall, 2002.

Zand, Dale E. *The Leadership Triad: Knowledge, Trust, and Power*. New York: Oxford University Press, 1997.

INDEX

About the Author

Jeswald W. Salacuse is Henry J. Braker Professor of Law at the Fletcher School of Law and Diplomacy, Tufts University, the senior graduate professional school of international affairs in the United States. From July 1986 to September 1994, Professor Salacuse served as The Fletcher School's Dean. He holds a J.D. from Harvard Law School, an A.B. from Hamilton College, and a diploma from the University of Paris. He has been a lecturer in law at Ahmadu Bello University in Nigeria, a lawyer with a Wall Street law firm, a professor of law, and director of research at the National School of Administration in the Congo, the Ford Foundation's Middle East advisor on law and development based in Beirut, Lebanon, and later the Foundation's representative in the Sudan. From 1980 to 1986, he served as Dean of the School of Law of Southern Methodist University. Professor Salacuse has traveled and lectured widely. He has been a Visiting Professor at the University of London, the University of Bristol, the Ecole Nationale des Ponts et Chaussées, Paris, and the Instituto de Empresa, Madrid. In the spring of 2000, he held the Fulbright Distinguished Chair in Comparative Law in Italy.

Professor Salacuse has written numerous books and articles, including *Making Global Deals: Negotiating in the International Marketplace* (1991, which has been translated into ten languages), *International Business Planning: Law and Taxation* (six volumes, with W. P. Streng),

An Introduction to Law in French-Speaking Africa (2 volumes), *Nigerian Family Law, The Art of Advice* (1994), and *The Wise Advisor: What Every Professional Should Know About Consulting and Counseling* (2000). His most recent book is *The Global Negotiator: Making, Managing, and Mending Deals Around the World in the Twenty-First Century* (2003).

Professor Salacuse has served as the Chairman of the Institute of Transnational Arbitration (1992–1994), Chairman of the Board of the Council for International Exchange of Scholars (1987–1991), President of the International Third World Legal Studies Association (1986–1991), and the founding President of the Association of Professional Schools of International Affairs (APSIA) (1988–1989). He has been a consultant to major multinational companies, government agencies, international organizations, universities, foundations, and foreign governments. He is a member of the Council on Foreign Relations and the American Law Institute, a Trustee of the Southwestern Legal Foundation, a member of the Steering Committee of the Program on Negotiation at Harvard Law School, and an independent director of several mutual funds.

41213958R00131

Made in the USA
Middletown, DE
08 March 2017